WHAT THEY DON'T TEACH AT SCHOOL

WHAT THEY DON'T TEACH AT SCHOOL

The Joy of Knowledge

Vijaya Khandurie

BLUEJAY

Bluejay Books Pvt. Ltd.
A-8/76, Ist Floor
Sector 16, Rohini
Delhi 110 085
info@bluejaybooksindia.com

First published in 2013 by
Bluejay Books Pvt. Ltd.

Typeset by EGP

Printed and bound in India

This small book is dedicated to
a great person – (Late) Dr. Subhash Chandra Sharma
(24.06.1951–20.02.2012):
a devoted son, a caring husband, a loving
father, a sincere friend, and above all,
a human being par excellence.

CONTENTS

PREFACE

General knowledge is an essential part of one's studies. There are hardly any competitions, exams, or even everyday transactions where general knowledge does not come in handy. Our young boys and girls, adults and senior people like to test their general awareness about the world and it is a matter of great pride that our students are doing very well in this field of knowledge and entertainment.

The present book is meant for everybody, especially students who want to test their general awareness and at the same time want to enhance it. The facts contained herein are fascinating and will open new vistas of information in varied fields of knowledge.

This quiz book is broadly divided into two parts – about India and the world. Efforts have been made to cover every possible topic. Suggestions from the readers will be highly appreciated.

June 2013
New Delhi

Vijaya Khandurie

INDIAN HISTORY

1. Out of which materials were crafted the famous toys of the Indus Valley Civilization?
   (a) Wood (b) Terracotta
   (c) Baked clay (d) Bronze

2. Which Director General of the Archaeological Survey of India was responsible for the excavation that led to the discovery of Harappa and Mohenjodaro, two of the main cities that comprise the Indus Valley Civilization?
   (a) William Jones (b) Alexander Cunningham
   (c) R .E.M. Wheeler (d) John Hubert Marshall

3. The Greeks called him Sandrocottus. He overthrew the Nanda rulers of Magadha and founded the Maurya Dynasty. Who was this great emperor who defeated Seleucus Nikator and expelled the Greeks from Punjab and Sind?
   (a) Bindusara (b) Samudragupta
   (c) Chandragupta (d) Kanishka

4. A great conqueror and patron of arts and literature, he expanded his empire from Bihar in the east, Ujjain in the west and Vindhyas in the south. Who was this great Kushan ruler who embraced and patronised Buddhism?
   (a) Ajat Shatru (b) Kanishka
   (c) Vishnugupta (d) Skandagupta

5. In the 4th century A.D., a powerful empire was set up in Magadha which later expanded to cover large area from north to south and lasted for three centuries. This period of which dynasty is known as the Golden Age in Indian history?
   (a) Kushan Dynasty (b) Maurya Dynasty
   (c) Vardhana Dynasty (d) Gupta Dynasty

6. Who in 1024 A.D. sacked the great Hindu religious center of Somnath, carrying away vast treasures after slaughtering more than fifty thousand people?
   (a) Muhammad Bin Qasim
   (b) Muhammad of Ghazni
   (c) Subuktagin
   (d) Muhammad Ghori

7. Razia Sultana, the eldest daughter of Iltutmish, was the first woman Muslim ruler of India whose rule lasted for only three-and-a-half years. She was dethroned on the pretext of her love for a slave by the name of Jalaluddin Yakub. From which place did this slave come?
   (a) Kandhar (b) Abyssinia
   (c) Mesopotamia (d) Mongolia

8. Which Rajput king founded Chittor and started guerrilla activities against the armies of Alauddin Khilji?
   (a) Hemu (b) Hamir
   (c) Rana Sanga (d) Rana Pratap

9. Around 151 B.C., Ashoka the Great, grandson of Chandragupta Maurya, waged a heinous war in which the terrible loss of human lives made him renounce all future wars. Against whom did Ashoka wage this battle?
   (a) Kushan (b) Kalinga
   (c) Kanishka (d) Kandhar

10. In the famous first battle of Tarain in 1191 A.D., which Rajput ruler of Delhi defeated Muhammad Ghauri, the Sultan of Ghazni?
    (a) Rana Sanga (b) Rana Pratap
    (c) Prithvi Raj Chauhan (d) Raja Man Singh

11. Which Hindu emperor was crushed to defeat by the allied forces of Ahmadnagar, Golkunda and Bihar on 26 January 1565, thereby disintegrating the empire?
    (a) Chandernagar (b) Maratha
    (c) Tanjore (d) Vijayanagar

12. Which ruler of Bengal was defeated by Robert Clive on 23 June 1756 at the Battle of Plassey?
    (a) Shuja-ud-daula (b) Siraj-ud-daula
    (c) Mir Jafer (d) Mir Qasim

13. In which battle in 1764 did the British forces led by Munro defeat both Mir Qasim and Shuja-ud-daula, thereby capturing Oudh?
    (a) Battle of Plassey (b) Battle of Murshidabad
    (c) Battle of Ramnagar (d) Battle of Buxar

14. In the fourth Mysore war, the British forces defeated Tipu Sultan, who died fighting in the war. Consequently, a part of his kingdom was annexed by the British and the rest given to the old Hindu dynasty. Who led the British forces against him?
    (a) Lord Hastings (b) Lord Cornwallis
    (c) Arthur Wellesley (d) William Bentines

15. The 1971 Indo-Pak war has not only created history, but geography as well when Pakistan army under General Niazi surrendered to Indian forces in Dhaka and a new nation—

Bangladesh—was formed. Who was the Chief of the Indian Army at that time?

(a) Gen. J.N. Choudhuri
(b) Gen. P.P. Kumarmangalam
(c) Gen. S.H.F.J. Manekshaw
(d) Gen. G.G. Bewoor

16. Which Mughal emperor was nick-named 'Rangila' because of his addiction to wine and women?

(a) Wajid Ali Shah (b) Mohammad Shah
(c) Ahmad Shah (d) Bahadur Shah

17. Which fort was captured by Akbar in 1568 wherein the Rajput women performed the rite of 'Jauhar', immolating themselves in order to be saved from dishonour?

(a) Ranthambor (b) Gwalior
(c) Jodhpur (d) Chittor

18. After eight years of confinement by his son Aurangzeb, where did Akbar breathe his last in January 1666?

(a) Agra Fort (b) Red Fort, Delhi
(c) Fatehpur Sikri (d) Sikandria

19. Who played the most crucial role in disintegrating the Mughal Empire?

(a) Rajputs (b) Marathas
(c) Rohillas (d) Peshwas

20. In which year was the East India Company granted Charter by Queen Elizabeth I to trade with east India?

(a) 1600 (b) 1610
(c) 1620 (d) 1630

21. Who was the Governor General of India at the time of Indian Independence?
    (a) Lord Willingdon (b) Lord Linlithgow
    (c) Lord Wavell (d) Lord Mountbatten

22. Who was the first and last Indian Governor General of India?
    (a) Sir Syed Ahmed Khan
    (b) General Maharaj Ranjit Singh
    (c) C. Rajagopalachari
    (d) M. Ananthasayanam Ayyangar

23. Where in Uttar Pradesh did the revolt of (10 May) 1857 begin?
    (a) Lucknow (b) Jhansi
    (c) Agra (d) Meerut

24. In a meeting with solders on 4 July 1944, the great patriot Subhash Chandra Bose uttered these words, "In this struggle for freedom, my friends, I am asking you for blood. You give me blood, I will give you freedom". Where in Myanmar (earlier Burma) did he make this speech?
    (a) Khayan (b) Thongwa
    (c) Yangon (d) Yandoon

25. Associated with the Kakori train dacoity case and known for his composition of '*Sarfaroshi ki tamanna ab hamare dil mein hai*…', which great patriot was hanged by the British?
    (a) Bhagat Singh (b) Ram Prasad Bismil
    (c) Mangal Pande (d) Khushi Ram

26. Which great Indian patriot succumbed to injuries inflicted during lathi-charge in a procession against the Simon Commission in 1928?
    (a) Bal Gangadhar Tilak (b) Lala Hardayal
    (c) Lala Lajpat Rai (d) Mangal Pande

27. Well-known as Ram Mohammad Singh 'Azadi', which revolutionary waited for twenty-one years after the Jalliyanwala Bagh massacre to take revenge with Gen. O'Dayer and shot him dead in an assembly in Cox Hall, London?
    (a) Sardar Udham Singh
    (b) Sardar Ajit Singh
    (c) Sardar Bhagat Singh
    (d) Sardar Kartar Singh Saraba

28. Which patriot uttered the following couplet before being hanged along with Bhagat Singh and Raj Guru on 23 March 1931: *"Dil se nikalegi na mar ke bhi watan ki ulfat,, meri mitti se bhi khushbhu-e-watan ayegi*?
    (a) Rajendra Lahiri   (b) Bhai Paramanand
    (c) Sukhdev   (d) Shah Nawaz

29. Which revolutionary was hanged in 1931 in Lahore Central Jail for killing Sounders, the then D.S.P. of Lahore?
    (a) Bhagat Singh   (b) Nirmal Ghosh
    (c) Awadh Behari   (d) Ras Behari Bos

30. Which brilliant student went to the USA to study, but engaged himself in revolutionary activities. He also, with the help of Baba Sohan Singh, formed the Ghadar Party in California in 1908?
    (a) Pt. Kashi Ram   (b) Keshav Singh
    (c) Lala Hardayal   (d) Veer Savarkar

31. He went abroad to study, but with a view to make India free from the British clutches. He joined the Ghadar Party later, only to be hanged in 1908 for the attempted murder of Kingsport, the then magistrate of Muzaffarpur. Identify the person.
    (a) Khudiram Bose   (b) Ras Bihar Bose
    (c) VasudevBasant Phadke   (d) Nirmal Ghosh

32. During the rule of which Governor General did the First War of Independence break out in 1857?
    1. LordWellesley 2. Lord Canning
    3. Lord Dalhousie 4. Lord Bentinck

33. Ram Prasad Bismil, Roshan Singh, Ashfaqulla Khan, and Rajindra Lahiri were hanged because of their involvement in the robbery of government treasury at Kakori. Which district of Uttar Pradesh is Kakori situated in?
    (a) Mainpuri (b) Balia
    (c) Lucknow (d) Sitapur

34. It was at Moirang on 12 February 1944 that the first Indian flag of the Indian Army was hoisted on Indian soil by Netaji Subhash Chandra Bose. In which state is Moirang situated?
    (a) Nagaland (b) Manipur
    (c) Mizoram (d) Tripura

35. Which among the following events gave rise to Indian National Movement after the First World War?
    (a) Gandhi Salt March
    (b) Jallianwala Massacre
    (c) Quit India Movement
    (d) Formation of Muslim League

36. In which year were the Portuguese possessions of Goa, Daman and Diu liberated by India?
    (a) 1960 (b) 1961
    (c) 1962 (d) 1963

37. Who was the Lieutenant Governor of Punjab when the Jallianwala Bagh massacre took place?
    (a) E. H. Dyer
    (b) Edward Douglas Maclagan
    (c) Louis William Dane
    (d) Michael Francis O'Dwyer

38. Who forwarded the idea of a separate homeland for the Muslims in the North-West in 1930?
    (a) Rahamat Ali (b) Mohammad Ali Jinnah
    (c) Mohammed Iqbal (d) Iskander Mirza

39. During the Mauryan era, which city was known as the gateway to the northwest, including Central Asia?
    (a) Harappa (b) Taxila
    (c) Kaushambhi (d) Kandhar

40. In which city of India did the East India Company make its first factory?
    (a) Surat (b) Baroda
    (c) Kolkata (d) Cuttack

HISTORY OF THE WORLD

☙

1. Which was the first colonial country in the world?
   (a) Britain (b) France
   (c) Portugal (d) Spain

2. Which country was the only non-European imperialistic power in the world?
   (a) Soudi Arabia (b) Mongolia
   (c) Korea (d) Japan

3. Thirteen colonies of Britain were the first to gain freedom. Which country did they form?
   (a) Australia (b) South Africa
   (c) USA (d) Canada

4. Which country was a Dutch colony for as many as three hundred and fifty years, from 1600 to 1949?
   (a) Malaya (b) Indonesia
   (c) Thailand (d) Laos

5. Which of the following countries did not colonise the Philippines?
   (a) Portugal (b) Spain
   (c) U.S.A. (d) Japan

6. Boers were the Dutch settlers in South Africa. What does the word 'boer' mean?
   (a) Soldier (b) Farmer
   (c) Fighter (d) Boxer

7. Which part of China was taken by the Britishers when they defeated China in the first Opium War?
   (a) Hechi (b) Taiwan
   (c) Formosa (d) Macau

8. Where in Virginia did the British colonialists establish the first colony in North America?
   (a) Jamestown (b) Georgetown
   (c) Plymouth (d) New Haven

9. Which British colony in North America became the first colony to recognize slavery as a legal institution in 1641?
   (a) Virginia (b) Massachusetts
   (c) South Carolina (d) Georgia

10. France was Europe's first country to abolish slavery in 1794. Identify the person who revived it in 1802?
    (a) Napoleon (b) Louis XIV
    (c) Philippe (d) Moselle

11. The first battle of the First World War was the Battle of Liege. Which country was invaded by Germany on 5 August 1914 resulting in Germany' victory?
    (a) Serbia (b) France
    (c) Belgium (d) Belgrade

12. The first Allied victory in the First World War was in the Battle of Cer from 16 to 19 August 1914. Which country was defeated by Serbia?
    (a) France (b) Austro-Hungary
    (c) Germany (d) Turkey

13. The German South Africa was conquered by combined forces of England and South Africa in battle that lasted for ten months. What is the present name of German South Africa?
    (a) Botswana (b) Congo
    (c) Namibia (d) Rhodesia

14. T.E. Lawrence was the British Commander in the Battle of Aqaba in which Arab rebels and the British troops trounced the Ottoman forces on 6 July 1917. What was T.E. Lawrence popularly known as?
    (a) Lawrence of Aqaba (b) Lawrence of Medina
    (c) Lawrence of Arabia (d) Lawrence of Nefud

15. Which date marked the end of the First World War with Germany, signing the Armistice of Compiègne?
    (a) 11 November 1918 (b) 15 November 1918
    (c) 25 November 1918 (d) 30 November 1918

16. Who was the last emperor of Russia from 1895 to 1917?
    (a) Alexander I (b) Alexander II
    (c) Nicholas I (d) Nicholas II

17. What was the name of the Russian Parliament which was introduced by Russian Tsar Nicholas II?
    (a) Duma (b) Milli Mejlis
    (c) Supreme Council (d) Majlisi Oli

18. Why was the 'October Revolution' of Russia called so, despite its taking place in November?
    (a) As per the Russian calendar
    (b) As per the Julian calendar
    (c) As per the Gregory calendar
    (d) Because October is the most pious month for the Russians

19. Which was Russia's first major battle in 1914 which led to the death of about 1,20,000 people?
    (a) Battle of Tannenberg (b) Battle of Kursk
    (c) Battle of the Bulge (d) Battle of the Coral Sea

20. Which among the following was the most significant event in the history of Italy between the two World Wars?
    (a) Rise of autocracy (b) Rise of Nazism
    (c) Rise of fascism (d) Crash of 1929

21. In which city of Italy did Benito Mussolini organize the fascist party on 23 March 1919?
    (a) Rome (b) Naples
    (c) Milan (d) Venice

22. Hitler's autobiography is titled *Mein Kampf*. What does it mean?
    (a) My Belief (b) My Struggle
    (c) My Objectives (d) My Determination

23. Which country was the first to be attacked by Germany, leading to the beginning of the World War Second on 1 September 1939?
    (a) Serbia (b) Austria
    (c) Bulgaria (d) Poland

24. What was the name of the German Air Force during Nazi's rule?
    (a) Firebombers (b) Mirage
    (c) Buccaneer (d) Luftwaffe

25. On which date did the Japanese forces attack the US Fleet at Pearl Harbour?
    (a) 7 December 1941 (b) 7 October 1941
    (c) 7 July 1941 (d) 7 March 1941

26. Who was the Prime Minister of Japan when Japan attacked Pearl Harbour on 7 December 1941?
    (a) Kantaro Suzuki (b) Shigenori Togo
    (c) Hideki Tojo (d) Fumimaro Kondoye

27. After the death of Sun Yat-sen in 1925, who assumed the leadership of the national government of the Republic of China (ROC) from 1928 to 1975?
    (a) Li Tsung-jen (b) Chiang Zhaocong
    (c) Chiang Kai-shek (d) Mao Fumei

28. In 1961, East Germany built a wall through the city of Berlin. What was the purpose of this Berlin Wall?
    (a) To prevent East Germans from emigrating to the West
    (b) To prevent West Germans to enter to the East
    (c) To prevent secrecy
    (d) All of these

29. In which year did West and East Germany unite to become Bundes Republik Deutschland (Federal Republic of Germany)?
    (a) 1970 (b) 1980
    (c) 1990 (d) 2000

30. Who was the first to use the phrase "Iron Curtain" for the Soviet Union in a speech delivered in Fulton, Missouri on 5 March 1946?
    (a) Roosevelt (b) Eisenhower
    (c) Churchill (d) Hitler

31. Which country did Julius Caeser conquere in the year 55 B.C.?
    (a) France (b) Greece
    (c) Britain (d) Austria

32. In which year did King John of England sign the famous Magna Carta to give more powers to the barons?
    (a) 1215 (b) 1225
    (c) 1235 (d) 1245

33. Which country did Britain fight against in the hundred year war starting from 1337 A.D.?
    (a) Spain (b) France
    (c) The Netherland (d) Sweden

34. Who was the President of the United States during the 1861-65 American civil war and was instrumental in banning slavery?
    (a) James Buchanan (b) Ulysses S. Grant
    (c) Andrew Johnson (d) Abraham Lincoln

35. Which of the following facts is not correct regarding the First World War?
    (a) The United States entered the war against Germany
    (b) The Soviet Union was formed
    (c) Nearly ten million people died in the war
    (d) None of these

36. What important event occured at the 11th hour of the 11th day of the 11th month of the year 1918?
    (a) Adolf Hitler formed his Nazi Party under the Swastik Flag
    (b) Russian Tsar Nicholas II was murdered
    (c) Birth of Soviet Union
    (d) The First World War officially ended

37. On which country was the First World War declared by the Germans in 1914?
    (a) Poland (b) Austria
    (c) France (d) Belgium

38. Which famous war was fought during the period 1965-1973?
    (a) The Korean War (b) The Vietnam War
    (c) The Falkland War (d) The Iran-Iraq War

39. In which year was the Berlin Wall torn down and Berlin united for the first time after World War II?
    (a) 1971 (b) 1979
    (c) 1989 (d) 1992

40. In which city of Pakistan did the American troops capture Osama bin Laden in 2011 and kill him?
    (a) Islamabad (b) Abbotabad
    (c) Peshawar (d) Jalalabad

GEOGRAPHY OF INDIA

1. Which land of yellow-soil in the Aravali Hills has a memorial pillar of Chetak, the faithful horse of Mahrana Pratap?
   (a) Chittor (b) Haldighati
   (c) Chittorgarh (d) Kumbhalgarh

2. Which district of West Bengal shares borders with three foreign countries?
   (a) Cooch Bihar (b) Jalpaiguri
   (c) Darjeeling (d) Murshidabad

3. Which among the following places has the highest rainfall in the world?
   (a) Mawsynram (b) Cherrapunji
   (c) Gowai (d) Maflong

4. At an attitude of 2286 m, which is the most famous hill state in Tamil Nadu which also houses Dodabeta, the highest peak in south India?
   (a) Kodaikanal (b) Mahabalipuram
   (c) Uthagamandalam (d) Kotagiri

5. Where can one find the Pinjor Garden, one of the oldest Mughal gardens?
   (a) Sri Nagar (b) Gulmarg
   (c) Pahalgam (d) Chandigarh

6. Where is the ruined fortress of Tipu Sultan located?
   (a) Belur (b) Halebid
   (c) Srirangapatam (d) Shringeri

7. Situated on the bank of river Shipra, the city was called Avantika in ancient times and was the capital of Chandragupta II. Name this city where the great poet Kalidasa composed his famous epic poems?
   (a) Khajuraho (b) Sanchi
   (c) Ujjain (d) Panchmarhi

8. Which industrial city on the banks of river Ganga is famous for textiles as also for the Sepoy Mutiny?
   (a) Allahabad (b) Meerut
   (c) Kanpur (d) Varanasi

9. Located on the valley of river Parvati at an attitude of 5700 ft, which place contains the hottest spring in the world?
   (a) Sahastradhara (b) Badrinath
   (c) Manali (d) Manikaran

10. Kavaratti is the capital of which Union territory of India?
    (a) Puducherry (b) Daman and Diu
    (c) Lakshdweep (d) Dadra and Nagar Haveli

11. Which is the largest district of India?
    (a) Mirzapur (b) Kuchchh
    (c) Ladakh (d) Warangal

12. Which is the largest state of India?
    (a) Rajasthan (b) Uttar Pradesh
    (c) Bihar (d) Madhya Pradesh

13. Which is the only National Capital Territory in India?
    (a) Chandigarh (b) Delhi
    (c) Goa (d) Puducherry

14. Which state of India does the Telangana Region come under?
    (a) Tamil Nadu (b) Karnataka
    (c) Gujarat (d) Andhra Pradesh

15. Where is the seat of High Court of Arunachal Pradesh situated?
    (a) Shillong (b) Dispur
    (c) Guwahati (d) Kohima

16. Where did the French have their headquarters in India?
    (a) Karaikal (b) Mahe
    (c) Yanam (d) Puducherry

17. Which state of India was Chhattisgarh carved out of?
    (a) Bihar (b) Uttar Pradesh
    (c) Madhya Pradesh (d) Rajasthan

18. How many states and Union Territories is India divided into?
    (a) 27 and 6 (b) 28 and 7
    (c) 28 and 6 (d) 29 and 7

19. Which Indian state is predominantly inhabited by the tribal people?
    (a) Bihar (b) Jharkhand
    (c) Chhattisgarh (d) Rajasthan

20. Which two provinces were bifurcated after the partition of India?
    (a) Punjab and Rajathan
    (b) Bengal and Jammu & Kashmir
    (c) Bengal and Punjab
    d) Punjab and Jammu & Kashmir

21. Which among the following is a cold desert?
    (a) Thar (b) Nefud
    (c) Arabian (d) Ladakh

22. In which state of India do these rivers flow: Siang, Lohit, Kameg, Dibang, and Kamlang?
    (a) Nagaland (b) Arunachal Pradesh
    (c) Meghalaya (d) Manipur

23. Which state houses the famous Loktak Lake?
    (a) Manipur (b) West Bengal
    (c) Assam (d) Odisha

24. Rivers Teesta and Rangit flow through which Indian state?
    (a) Goa (b) Kerala
    (c) Sikkim (d) Himachal Pradesh

25. In which Union Territory of India are Rossiland and Havelock islands situated?
    (a) Poducherry (b) Dadra and Nagar Haveli
    (c) Lakshadweep (d) Andaman and Nicobar

26. Which boundary separates Andaman from Nicobar islands?
    (a) McMahon Line (b) Durand Line
    (c) Radcliffe Line (d) Ten-Degree Channel

27. Which is the smallest Union Territory in India?
    (a) Poducherry (b) Dadra and Nagar Haveli
    (c) Lakshadweep (d) Daman and Diu

28. Which is the largest fresh water lake in India?
    (a) Wular Lake (b) Chilka Lake
    (c) Dal Lake (d) Lake Jaisamand

29. Where is the southernmost place in India, i.e. Indira Point located?

    (a) Kerala (b) Tamil Nadu

    (c) Andaman Island (d) Great Nicobar Island

30. Which country does India share the least land border with?

    (a) Bhutan (b) Afghanistan

    (c) Myanmar (d) Nepal

GEOGRAPHY OF THE WORLD

1. At what angle is the Tropic of Cancer inclined?
   (a) 66½° N (b) 66½° S
   (c) 23½° S (d) 23½° N

2. The branch of sociology that studies the characteristics of human populations is called:
   (a) Cartography (b) Paleography
   (c) Hagiography (d) Demography

3. What is popularly known as the molten rock in the earth's crust?
   (a) Lava (b) Agma
   (c) Magma (d) Syntagma

4. Which Japanese word means "Harbour waves"?
   (a) Tsushima (b) Tsunami
   (c) Tsukahara (d) Tsinghai

5. Which layer of Earth's atmosphere helps in radio transmission?
   (a) Exosphere (b) Photosphere
   (c) Centrosphere (d) Thermosphere

6. What was Mt. Everest earlier known as?
   (a) Crest XV (b) Summit XV
   (c) Peak XV (d) Tip XV

7. Which German mapmaker made the first known globe called the *erdapfel,* i.e. the earth apple?
   (a) Martin Behaim (b) Charles Hoffmann
   (c) Karl Spruner von Merz (d) Matthäus Seutter

8. Which is an imaginary line which runs from the North Pole to the South Pole, and through main telescope at the Royal Observatory in Greenwich?
   (a) 180° Latitude (b) 180° Longitude
   (c) Zero Latitude (d) Zero Longitude

9. Which major European river carries more traffic than any other river in the world?
   (a) Rhone (b) Volga
   (c) Po (d) Seine

10. Which river rises in Tibet, then flows through northern India and unites in the Arabian Sea?
   (a) Jhelum (b) Indus
   (c) Irawadi (d) Brahmputra

11. Which mountains range lies between France and Switzerland?
   (a) Alps (b) Jura
   (c) Bernina (d) Harz

12. What is the term used to describe a long narrow inlet of the sea between steep cliffs, common in Norway?
   (a) Fjord (b) Estuary
   (c) Calanque (d) Ria

13. What you call a pass between mountain peaks?
   (a) Col (b) Saddle
   (c) Defile (d) Notch

14. Which is the main river of Myanmar which empties into the Andaman Sea?
    (a) Thanlwin (b) Chindwin
    (c) Irawadi (d) Sittaung

15. After Nanda Devi, which is the second highest mountain in the Garhwal region of India?
    (a) Kamet (b) Trisul 1
    (c) Swargarohini (d) Nilkanth

16. Which 16th century geographer invented a type of projection of maps of the globe and was the first to use the term *Atlas*?
    (a) Diogo Ribeiro (b) Karl Siemon
    (c) Johann Lambert (d) Gerardus Mercator

17. Which cardinal compass point is at 0 or 360 degrees?
    (a) North (b) East
    (c) West (d) South

18. Which part of a Union Territory of India was discovered in 1498 by Vasco de Gama?
    (a) Diu (b) Daman
    (c) Dadra (d) Nagar Haveli

19. In which country can one find the Nagev desert?
    (a) Mongolia (b) Israel
    (c) Jordan (d) Chad

20. What is the term used for a landform that is created at the mouth of a river where that river flows into a water body?
    (a) Bight (b) Strait
    (c) Delta (d) Coast

21. Name the mountain range in central Asia where Russia, China, Mongolia and Kazakhstan meet?
    (a) Ural (b) Altai
    (c) Tian Shan (d) Zagros

22. Which term is used to describe a submerged ridge of rock or coral near the surface of water?
    (a) Reef (b) Atoll
    (c) Wadi (d) Arete

23. Which is the largest island in the West Indies?
    (a) Bahamas (b) Barbados
    (c) Grenada (d) Cuba

24. Which Asian river between China and Russia flows into the Sea of Okhotsk?
    (a) Ussuri (b) Amur
    (c) Bureya (d) Songhua

25. Which is the longest river in France?
    (a) Loire (b) Seine
    (c) Rhone (d) Rhine

26. Which State of Malaysia holds the world's second largest tropical rainforest after the Amazon?
    (a) Malacca (b) Pahang
    (c) Penang (d) Sarawak

27. Which mountain range in South America runs five thousand miles along the Pacific coast?
    (a) Sierra de Velasco (b) Andes
    (c) Cordon Baquedano (d) Cordillera del Paine

28. Name a small island in the central Pacific Ocean whose economy depends on phosphate exports?
    (a) Guam (b) Kiribati
    (c) Nauru (d) Papua New Guinea

29. Which small principality is located in the Alps between Austria and Switzerland?
    (a) Andorra (b) Asturias
    (c) Malta (d) Liechtenstein

30. Which is the longest river in England that flows eastward through London to the North Sea?
    (a) Thames (b) Ellen
    (c) Greta (d) Keer

INDIAN CONSTITUTION

1. On which date did the Constituent Assembly pass the Constitution of India?
   (a) 22.1.1947 (b) 26.9.1948
   (c) 26.11.1949 (d) 26.1.1950

2. When did the Constitution of India come into effect?
   (a) 15.8.1947 (b) 26.9.1948
   (c) 26.11.1949 (d) 26.1.1950

3. Who was the Chairman of the Drafting Committee?
   (a) Frank Anthony (b) K.M. Munshi
   (c) B.R. Ambedkar (d) H.P. Modi

4. The general structure of the Constitution's democratic framework was largely the work of which constitutional expert?
   (a) B. N. Rau (b) Alladi Krishnaswamy Iyer
   (c) Hansa Mehta (d) B.R.Ambedkar

5. Which of the following features of the Indian Constitution was not adapted from the British Constitution?
   (a) Parliamentary form of government
   (b) The idea of single citizenship
   (c) Federal structure of government
   (d) Institution of Speaker and his role

6. Which great American President once said about democracy: "...the government of the people, by the people and for the people."?
   (a) George Washington (b) James Buchanan
   (c) Woodrow Wilson (d) Abraham Loncoln

7. Who among the following was the only to be chosen as President for two terms?
   (a) Dr. S. Radhakrishnan (b) Dr. Rajendra Prasad
   (c) V.V. Giri (d) Neelam Sanjeev Reddy

8. Which two Ministries are located in the North Block situated at Raisina Hill, Delhi?
   (a) Finance and Home (b) Defence and Finance
   (c) Home and Defence (d) Railways and Defence

9. Established in 1862, which two High Courts among the following are the oldest in India?
   (a) Bombay and Madras (b) Madras and Calcutta
   (c) Bombay and Mysore (d) Bombay and Calcutta

10. Who was the first President to die while holding the office?
    (a) Fakhruddin Ali Ahmed (b) Dr. Zakir Hussain
    (c) Gyani Zail Singh (d) Dr. Shankar Dayal Sharma

11. Which among the following Vice Presidents did not become the President?
    (a) Dr. Zakir Hussain (b) V.V. Giri
    (c) K.R. Narayanan (d) G.S. Pathak

12. Who was the only Chief Justice of the Supreme Court of India to become the Vice President of India?
    (a) G.S. Pathak (b) Krishan Kant
    (c) M.H.Baig (d) M. Hidaytullah

13. Who was the first Speaker of the Lok Sabha?
    (a) G.V. Mavlankar (b) M.A. Ayyangar
    (c) B.R. Bhagat (d) Sardar Hukum Singh

14. Who was the first Chief Justice of the Supreme Court of India?
    (a) S.R. Das (b) K. Subba Rao
    (c) M.H. Kania (d) H.J. Kania

15. What is the maximum number of Members of the Rajya Sabha?
    (a) 250 (b) 300
    (c) 350 (d) 400

16. How many members can be nominated for Lok Sabha by the President for the Anglo-Indian Community?
    (a) 1 (b) 2
    (c) 3 (d) 4

17. How many Members are nominated by the President for the Rajya Sabha?
    (a) 10 (b) 11
    (c) 12 (d) 13

18. In the Parliament, the Question Hour is:
    (a) The first hour of sitting in both the Houses
    (b) Preceded by the Zero Hour
    (c) The first hour after the lunch break
    (d) The last hour of the day

19. During the Question Hour, a starred (*) question is the one which:
    (a) A member desires an oral answer from the Minister
    (b) Requires a written answer
    (c) Is not mandatory to be answered
    (d) Can be answered in writing any time before the end of the Session

20. Who can resolve the disputes between the Union and State?
    (a) President of India (b) Prime Minister of India
    (c) Attorney General (d) Supreme Court of India

21. Which Indian state has the largest reserved Lok Sabha seats?
    (a) Bihar (b) Madhya Pradesh
    (c) Uttar Pradesh (d) Rajasthan

22. Which of the following is not among the three-tier structure of the Panchayat Raj?
    (a) Gram Panchayat (b) Panchayat Samiti
    (c) Zila Parishad (d) Rajya Parishad

23. Which is the major source of income of the Panchayat Samiti?
    (a) Share in the land revenue collected by the government
    (b) Income on common land
    (c) Grants-in-Aid by the State Government
    (d) Taxes from the property

24. Which of the following is not a member of the Zila Parishad?
    (a) Member of the Legislative Assembly
    (b) Member of the Parliament
    (c) A representative of the Cooperative Society
    (d) A representative of the Rashtrapati Bhawan

25. Who presides the General Council of the Municipal Corporation?
    (a) Commissioner (b) Lt. Governor
    (c) Speaker (d) Mayor

26. Who represents the interests of the State in court?
    (a) Defence lawyer
    (b) Lawyer of the complainant
    (c) Station House Officer
    (d) Public Prosecutor

27. According to the Indian Constitution, which among the following is not an organ of the State?
    (a) Election Commission (b) Legislature
    (c) Executive (d) Judiciary

28. What is the highest number of candidates that an electronic voting machine can support?
    (a) 36 (b) 48
    (c) 64 (d) 72

29. Who was the first woman Chief Minister of any state of India?
    (a) Nandini Satpathy (b) Sashikala Kadokar
    (c) Sucheta Kriplani (d) J. Jayalalitha

30. From which Constitution was the concept of a Five Year Plan borrowed into the Indian Constitution?
    (a) USSR (b) UK
    (c) Japan (d) Ireland

NATIONAL AND INTERNATIONAL ORGANISATIONS

1. Established on 16 October 1945 in Quebec City, Canada, where can one find the headquarters of the Food and Agriculture Organisation (FAO) since 1951?
   (a) Montreal (b) Washington D. C.
   (c) Rome (d) Geneva

2. For which international agency was Mohamed El Baradei of Egypt awarded the Nobel Peace Prize in 2005?
   (a) Unrepresented Nations and Peoples Organisation (UNPO)
   (b) World Meteorological Organisation (WMO)
   (c) United Nations Educational, Scientific and Cultural Organisation (UNESCO)
   (d) International Atomic Energy Agency (IAEA)

3. Which became the first specialized agency of the newly formed United Nations in 1946?
   (a) International Labour Organisation
   (b) United Nations High Commissioner for Human Rights
   (c) United Nations High Commissioner for Refugees
   (d) World Food Programme

4. Where are the headquarters of the World Health Organisation (WHO) situated?
   (a) Paris (b) Geneva
   (c) Zurich (d) London

5. Which organisation was founded in Cairo in 1945 by six countries – Egypt, Iraq, Lebanon, Saudi Arabia, Syria, and Transjordan (now Jordan)?
   (a) Group of Arab Unity
   (b) Gulf Cooperation Council
   (c) Arab League
   (d) Arab Maghreb Union

6. What do the letters "I" and "E" in the acronym UNICEF stand for (United Nations I… Children's E….Fund)?
   (a) International; Educational
   (b) International; Emergency
   (c) Immediate; Emergency
   (d) Immediate; Economic

7. Since 2008, which international organisation is Kamlesh Sharma of India the Secretary General of?
   (a) Commonwealth of Nations
   (b) Indian Ocean Commission
   (c) World Tourism Organisation
   (d) Asian Development Bank

8. Which of the following countries is not a member of the G8 (Group of Eight), the governments of eight of the world's largest economies?
   (a) Canada (b) Italy
   (c) Russia (d) Saudi Arabia

9. Originally, BRIC (an association of emerging national economies) consisted of Brazil, Russia, India and China. In 2010, another country was included in it and it became BRICS. What does "S" indicate?
   (a) Saudi Arabia (b) South Korea
   (c) South Africa (d) Switzerland

10. Association of Southeast Asian Nations (ASEAN) is a geo-political and economic organization of ten countries of Southeast Asia. Where in Indonesia did the first ASEAN summit take place on 23-24 February 1976?
    (a) Bali (b) Jakarta
    (c) Bandung (d) Sumatra

11. Where are the headquarters of the International Monetary Fund (IMF) located?
    (a) New York City (b) Washington D.C.
    (c) Berne (d) Berlin

12. Jacques Rogge is the President of the International Olympic Committee since 2001. To which country does he belong?
    (a) Germany (b) Austria
    (c) Belgium (d) Switzerland

13. In the acronym CONCACAF (Confederation of North, Central American and Caribbean A..., what do the letters "A" and "F" stand for?
    (a) American Fareast (b) African Federation
    (c) Agriculture Farmers (d) Association Football

14. Jim Yong Kim of South Korea is the President of which financial institution since 2012?
    (a) World Bank (b) Asian Development Bank
    (c) World Bank Group
    (d) International Finance Corporation

15. Where are the headquarters of the North Atlantic Treaty Organization (NATO) signed on 4 April 1949?
    (a) Amsterdam (b) Brussels
    (c) Copenhagen (d) Luxembourg

16. The Non-Aligned Movement (NAM) was founded in Belgrade in 1961. Who was the first to give the idea of this doctrine at the United Nations in 1953?
    (a) Josip Broz Tito (b) Gamal Abdel Nasser
    (c) Jawaharlal Nehru (d) V.K. Krishnamenon

17. Who among the following Indians was once the Chairperson of the Non-Aligned Movement?
    (a) Gyani Zail Singh (b) Jawaharlal Nehru
    (c) Indira Gandhi (d) Morarji Desai

18. Who was the first to coin the term "United Nations" as a term to describe the Allied countries?
    (a) Winston Churchill (b) D.W. Eisenhower
    (c) Trygve Lie (d) Franklin D. Roosevelt

19. Which Secretary General of the United Nations passed away in an air-crash while holding the office? He was also the only person to get a Nobel Prize posthumously.
    (a) U Thant (b) Kurt Waldheim
    (c) Dag Hammarskjold (d) Javier Perez de Cuellar

20. Where are the headquarters of the International Court of Justice located?
    (a) Stockholm (b) The Hague
    (c) Milan (d) Budapest

21. Which among the following facts is not correct about the European Union (EU)?
    (a) The European Parliament is elected by EU citizens every five years
    (b) The *de fact* capital of EU is Brussels
    (c) The EU was awarded the Nobel Peace Prize in 2012
    (d) There are thirty member States in the EU

22. Where are the headquarters of the International Federation of Association Football (FIFA) situated? This federation governs the association football, futsal and beach soccer throughout the world?
    (a) Zurich (b) Paris
    (c) Madrid (d) Amsterdam

23. Which international cricket organization is based in Dubai, United Arab Emirates?
    (a) The Asian Cricket Council (ACC)
    (b) The Gulf Cricket Association (GCA)
    (c) The International Cricket Council (ICC)
    (d) The Mideast Cricket Council (MECC)

24. Who was instrumental in founding the International Committee of the Red Cross in 1863? It is one of the oldest, most honoured and widely recognized organizations in the world, having won three Nobel Peace Prizes in 1917, 1944, and 1963?
    (a) Karen Tenenbaum (b) Doctor Massimo Barra
    (c) Gail J. McGovern (d) Henry Dunant

25. Which among the following organizations is not based at Geneva, Switzerland?
    (a) The World Meteorological Organization
    (b) Universal Postal Union
    (c) The World Intellectual Property Organization
    (d) The International Standards Organization

26. Founded on 15 September 1883, which organization, one of the largest in India, is engaged in conservation and biodiversity research?
    (a) Green Movement in India
    (b) Nature Conservation Foundation
    (c) Salim Ali Centre for Ornithology and Natural History
    (d) Bombay Natural History Society

27. In which year was the Rashtriya Swayamsevak Sangh (RSS) founded by Dr. K.B. Hedgewar to counter both British colonialism in India and Muslim separatism?
    (a) 1925 (b) 1935
    (c) 1945 (d) 1955

28. Constituted on 12 October 1993, which organization in India is responsible for the protection and promotion of human rights guaranteed by the Constitution of India?
    (a) United Christian Forum for Human Rights
    (b) People's Union for Civil Liberties
    (c) National Human Rights Commission
    (d) Confederation of Human Rights Organizations

29. Where is the Consumer Guidance Society of India located? It was founded in 1966 by a group of nine women for testing the purity of food products, weights and measures used by shopkeepers, and consumer protection in other forms?
    (a) New Delhi (b) Kolkata
    (c) Nagpur (d) Mumbai

30. Which sporting club in India is the 'birthplace' of the Chinese style dish by the name *Chicken Manchurian* which was 'invented' by Nelson Wang while working as a cook for that club?
    (a) National Sports Club of India
    (b) The Cricket Club of India
    (c) The Calcutta Swimming Club
    (d) Royal Bombay Yacht Club

ECONOMY AND BUSINESS

1. Which is the largest Bank in India?
   - (a) Corporation Bank
   - (b) Central Bank of India
   - (c) State Bank of India
   - (d) Punjab and Sind Bank

2. Established as "The Native Share & Stock Brokers Association" in 1875, which is the largest Stock Exchange in India?
   - (a) Delhi Stock Exchange, Delhi
   - (b) National Stock Exchange of India, Mumbai
   - (c) Inter-connected Stock Exchange of India, Mumbai
   - (d) Bombay Stock Exchange, Mumbai

3. Which is India's largest automobile company?
   - (a) Tata Motors
   - (b) Mahindra & Mahindra
   - (c) Premier
   - (d) Force

4. Who was independent India's first Finance Minister?
   - (a) John Mathai
   - (b) R. K. Shanmukham Chetty
   - (c) Chintamanrao Deshmukh
   - (d) T.T. Krishnamchari

5. Which city in U.P. is most famous for glass bangles?
   - (a) Firozabad
   - (b) Faizabad
   - (c) Faridabad
   - (d) Fatehpur

6. Ludhiana in Punjab is famous for which of the following products?
   - (a) Hosiery & Silk
   - (b) Hosiery & Cycle
   - (c) Cycle & leather products
   - (d) Silk & electric goods

7. Which place in India is most famous for ship-building?
   (a) Goa (b) Tiruvanantpuram
   (c) Kochi (d) Visakhapatnam

8. Situated on the bank of river Noyyal in Tamil Nadu, which is known as the'knitwear capital' of India, because of its ₹220 billion market in textile industry?
   (a) Salem (b) Tirupur
   (c) Trichy (d) Madurai

9. Which is the largest economic sector of the socio-economic development of India?
   (a) Railways (b) Tourism
   (c) Agriculture (d) Service

10. What is India's ranking in the world in production of milk, pulses and jute?
   (a) First (b) Second
   (c) Third (d) Fourth

11. During the reign of Prime Minister Indira Gandhi, how many banks were nationalised in 1969?
   (a) 10 (b) 12
   (c) 14 (d) 16

12. Which among the following companies is privately owned in petroleum industry in India?
   (a) Oil and Natural Gas Corporation
   (b) Hindustan Petroleum Corporation Limited
   (c) Oil Corporation Limited
   (d) Reliance Industries Limited

13. Which among the following elements available in India constitutes one-fourth of world's reserves that will help India further her nuclear energy program in future?
   (a) Thorium (b) Uranium
   (c) Platinum (d) Cobalt

14. Having a railway track length of about 65,000 km, what is the ranking of Indian Railway in the world?
    (a) First (b) Second
    (c) Third (d) Fourth

15. Which among the following denominations is ceased to be legal currency in India with effect from 30 June 2011?
    (a) Five paise (b) Ten paise
    (c) Twenty paise (d) All the above

16. Which of the following countries is the biggest importer of Indian products?
    (a) Singapore (b) The U. S. A.
    (c) China (d) United Arab Emirates

17. Which country out of the following is India's largest trading partner?
    (a) China (b) United Arab Emirates
    (c) U. S. A. (d) Saudi Arabia

18. Which political party is associated with All India Trade Union Congress?
    (a) Indian National Congress
    (b) Revolutionary Socialist Party
    (c) All India Forward Bloc
    (d) Communist Party of India

19. Which President of India was once the Finance Minister of India too?
    (a) R. Venkataraman
    (b) Varahagiri Venkata Giri
    (c) Neelam Sanjiva Reddy
    (d) Shankar Dayal Sharma

20. Regarded as the "100 most influential persons in the world" by *Time Magazine*, which Nobel Prize winner is best known for his work on the causes of famine and for his contributions to welfare economics?
    (a) Amartya Sen (b) Gary Becker
    (c) Merton Miller (d) Franco Modigliani

21. Which ountry is the biggest producer of wheat and rice?
    (a) U. S. A. (b) India
    (c) China (d) Russia

22. India is the largest producer in the world of which of the following fruits?
    (a) Banana (b) Papaya
    (c) Lemon (d) All the above

23. Which country has the world's largest proven reserves of oil, 20% of the world's proved oil reserves?
    (a) Russia (b) U. S. A.
    (c) Saudi Arabia (d) China

24. Which country leads the world by producing one-fourth of the world's total production of wool?
    (a) China (b) Australia
    (c) Brazil (d) South Africa

25. Who was the first President of the World Bank?
    (a) Robert McNamara (b) Eugene R. Black, Sr.
    (c) John J. McCloy (d) Eugene Meyer

26. Which country was the first to receive financial aid from the World Bank?
    (a) France (b) Poland
    (c) Chile (d) Ivory Coast

27. According to *Forbes* magazine, which country is the richest in the world as per gross domestic product (GDP) at purchasing power parity per capita?
    (a) Qatar (b) Luxembourg
    (c) Singapore (d) Norway

28. Which is the most expensive nation in the world to live in?
    (a) Finland (b) Denmark
    (c) Norway (d) Switzerland

29. Author of book *Capitalism and Freedom*, which Nobel Laureate in Economics is the most influential economist of the 20th century?
    (a) Jan Tinbergen (b) Gunnar Myrdal
    (c) Milton Friedman (d) James Heckman

30. Which Canadian-American economist and author of *The Affluent Society* said, "Economics is extremely useful as a form of employment for economists"?
    (a) James Buchanan (b) Henry Hazlitt
    (c) Julian L. Simon (d) John Kenneth Galbraith

RELIGIONS

1. Where was Shri Satya Sai Baba born on 23 November 1926?
   (a) Shirdi (b) Dharmavaram
   (c) Anantpur (d) Puttaparthi

2. Which beautiful hill station houses the famous Dilwara temples?
   (a) Udaipur (b) Jodhpur
   (c) Mount Abu (d) Jaisalmer

3. Which Sikh guru laid the foundation of the city of Amritsar in 1579?
   (a) Guru Arjun Das (b) Guru Ram Das
   (c) Guru Gobind Singh (d) Guru Angad Dev

4. About 2500 years ago, under a peepul tree in a small village Urubillwa, Gautam Buddha attained salvation. By what name is this village known today?
   (a) Sarnath (b) Gaya
   (c) Bodh Gaya (d) Mahabodhi

5. The word 'Veda' means 'knowledge' and a collection of hymns, prayers and invocations. Which of the four 'Vedas' is the earliest and assembled to be the oldest literature of the world?
   (a) Rig Veda (b) Sama Veda
   (c) Yajur Veda (d) Atharva Veda

6. Apart from being a holy man, he was a general who militarised the Sikh movement, and political leader who first fought with Bahadur Shah, then turned against him. Who was this Sikh Guru and the saviour of Hinduism who was stabbed by a Pathan in Novermber 1708?

   (a) Guru Teg Bahadur (b) Guru Arjan Das
   (c) Guru Gobind Singh (d) Raja Ranjit Singh

7. In which language did Buddha give his sermons?

   (a) Sanskrit (b) Pali
   (c) Prakrit (d) Brahmi

8. Which animal does the *ashvamedha* sacrifice pertain to?

   (a) Goat (b) Elephant
   (c) Mule (d) Horse

9. After attaining enlightenment, where did the Buddha go for preaching?

   (a) Sanchi (b) Bodhgaya
   (c) Sarnath (d) Varanasi

10. Where did the Buddha breathe his last?

    (a) Kasinara (b) Pokhara
    (c) Mansarovar (d) Sanchi

11. What was the name of Buddha's wife?

    (a) Yashodhara (b) Maya
    (c) Gargi (d) Sulochana

12. The tomb of the most revered Muslim sufi saint Muinuddin Chishti is the main attraction of which city in Rajasthan?

    (a) Alwar (b) Ajmer
    (c) Kota (d) Udaipur

13. Zoroastrians are the follower of which great Iranian spiritual teacher who lived about 1500 B.C.?
    (a) Ovadia Yosef (b) Sayyed Ali Khamenei
    (c) Ibrahim al-barmawi (d) Zarathrustra

14. Name the biggest Hindu temple in the world?
    (a) Wat Rong Khun, Thailand
    (b) Angkor Wat, Cambodia
    (c) Prambanan temple, Indonesia
    (d) Vishnu Temple Srirangam, Trichy

15. From which country did the pioneering Roman Catholic missionary Jesuit Francis Xavier come to Goa in 1542 on a mission to spread the gospel?
    (a) Spain (b) Portugal
    (c) Italy (d) Albania

16. Which religion initiated by Akbar, had an objective to unite the people of his empire?
    (a) Ahmadiyya (b) Din-i-Ilahi
    (c) Yazdanism (d) Karaimism

17. Where did Adi Shankaracharya, the great Hindu reformer, establish his *ashram*?
    (a) Badrinath (b) Kedarnath
    (c) Puri (d) Madurai

18. Where is Dargah Shareef, one of the most important centres of Muslim pilgrimage situated?
    (a) Ajmer (b) Fatehpur Sikri
    (c) Agra (d) Sikandarabad

19. Tirupati houses one of the most famous temples in India. In which state is its main temple Tirumala located?
    (a) Karnataka (b) Kerala
    (c) Tamil Nadu (d) Andhra Pradesh

20. Where is the Basilica of Bom Jesus situated?
    (a) Dadar Nagar Haveli (b) Tamil Nadu
    (c) Goa (d) Podduchery

21. Which country has the largest population of Muslims in the world?
    (a) Bangladesh (b) Pakistan
    (c) India (d) Indonesia

22. Khwaja Moinuddin Chishti was the first major Sufi teacher to come to India and settle in Ajmer. Where did he breathe his last?
    (a) Mysore (b) Medina
    (c) Fatehpur Sikri (d) Delhi

23. Which form of Muslim faith did Ghulam Ahmad of Qadian initiate in 1879?
    (a) Ahmadiya (b) Bahai
    (c) Parsi (d) Yazdanism

24. Where did the Dalai Lama, the spiritual head of Tibet, establish his monastery?
    (a) Mussoorie (b) Manali
    (c) Dharamshala (d) Dalhousie

25. What is the holiest day of the year for the inhabitants of Israel?
    (a) Yom Kippur (b) Rosh Hashana
    (c) Hanukkah (d) Yom HaAtzmaut

26. Which among the following poet-saints and devotees of Lord Krishna was visually impaired?
    (a) Kabirdas (b) Surdas
    (c) Tulsidas (d) Ravidas

27. Who among the following was one of the greatest poet-saints of Maharashtra?
    (a) Dadu Dayal (b) Tyagaraj
    (c) Haridas (d) Tukaram

28. Built by Fariborz Sahba, a Bahai architect, the Bahai Temple is a unique architectural wonder of the modern times. Which flower does it resemble in shape?
    (a) Gladioli (b) Tulips
    (c) Rose (d) Lotus

29. Which famous temple was built by Narasimha I during 1230-58 A.D.?
    (a) Papanath Temple (Tamil Nadu)
    (b) Mahabalipuram Temple (Tamil Nadu)
    (c) The Sun Temple, Konark (Orissa)
    (d) Lakshmana Temple, Khajuraho (M.P.)

30. Where is the Santhom Cathedral situated?
    (a) Chennai (b) Mumbai
    (c) Kolkata (d) Goa

INDIAN HERITAGE AND CULTURE

1. Which north Indian festival marks the beginning of the spring season on the fifth day of the waxing moon of Magh, marked with people wearing clothes in bright shades of yellow?
   (a) Vasant Panchami (b) Nag Panchami
   (c) Navratri (d) Ganesh Chaturthi

2. Where in Uttar Pradesh is the famous 'Nauchandi Mela' celebrated, known for active participation by both Hindus and Muslims?
   (a) Aligarh (b) Garhmukteshwar
   (c) Haridwar (d) Meerut

3. Which type of religious songs of devotion were composed by Tulsidas, Meerabai, Kabir and Surdas?
   (a) Shloka (b) Kirtan
   (c) Aarti (d) Bhajan

4. Which festival is celebrated to mark the end of Ramzan, the Muslim month of fasting?
   (a) Id-ul-Milad (b) Id-ul-Zuha
   (c) Id-ul-Fitr (d) Muharram

5. Which type of necklace consisting of emerald and ruby pendant held by pearl strands is worn only by the married south Indian women as a mark of being married?
   (a) Karnaphool Jhumka
   (b) Paizeb
   (c) Mangalsutra
   (d) Linga Padakka Muthu Malai

6. Which tribe of Meghalaya celebrates their five-day long most important festival 'Ka Ponblang Nongrem'?
   (a) Bodo (b) Deori
   (c) Khasi (d) Kuki

7. Which is the most important festival of the Jain community?
   (a) Paryushana Parva (b) Mahamastakabhisheka
   (c) Gyana Panchami (d) Mahavir Jayanti

8. Jamshed-e-Navroz is the most important festival of which Indian community?
   (a) Ahmadiyyas (b) Parsis
   (c) Moplahs (d) Jews

9. Which is the most popular festival of Kerala?
   (a) Vishu (b) Pongal
   (c) Onam (d) Deepavali

10. The 3-day long festival 'Moru Utsav' is exclusively held in which city of Rajasthan?
    (a) Bikaner (b) Jaisalmer
    (c) Udaipur (d) Kota

11. Which famous festival is celebrated in Ujjain, Nashik, Hardwar, and Allahabad?
    (a) Shiv Ratri (b) Janmashthami
    (c) Kumbh Mela (d) Rath Yatra

12. One of the oldest surviving theatre traditions of the world is 'Kutiyattam'. From which state of India did it originate some 2,000 year back?
    (a) Kerala (b) Tamil Nadu
    (c) Karnataka (d) Andhra Pradesh

13. Which eminent India-born musician is the conductor of world famous Israel Philharmonic Orchestra and New York Philharmonic Orchestra?
    (a) Orun Coomar Gangoly (b) Ramesh Sanzgiri
    (c) Zubin Mehta (d) Jayarama Iyer

14. Kathi, Chhau, Baul, Jatra, and Lama are the folk dances of which of the Indian states?
    (a) Odisha (b) Assam
    (c) Mizoram (d) West Bengal

15. Which among the following folk dances does not belong to Karnataka?
    (a) Jhakura (b) Hattari
    (c) Yakshagana (d) Suggi Kunitha

16. 'Gidda' is the women's dance from which Indian state?
    (a) Gujarat (b) Rajasthan
    (c) Haryana (d) Punjab

17. Dhela, Maru, and Chakri are the folk dances of which Indian state?
    (a) Madhya Pradesh (b) Uttarakhand
    (c) Rajasthan (d) Jharkhand

18. Which musical instrument in the form of a set of small brass bells is an accessory used by performers of all classical dances?
    (a) Manjeera (b) Kanjeera
    (c) Ghungroo (d) Kartal

19. Which Indian string musical instrument has a hollow body and consists of forty strings of which thirty-seven are sympathetic?
    (a) Veena (b) Saraswati Veena
    (c) Sarangi (d) Sarod

20. Sonal Mansingh is an exponent of which style of classical dance?
    (a) Kathak (b) Odissi
    (c) Kathakali (d) Bharatnatyam

21. Raja and Radha Reddy are a world-renowned dancing couple in this Indian classical dance form:
    (a) Kuchipudi (b) Bharatnatyam
    (c) Kathakali (d) Kathak

22. A dance-drama form that originated in Kerala, is characterized by its complicated language of mime and colorful makeup that resemble masks:
    (a) Kalaripayattu (b) Yakshgana
    (c) Kathakali (d) Mohiniyattam

23. Sitara Devi, Shambhu Maharaj, and Yamini Krishnamurthi are exponents of which style of Indian classical dance?
    (a) Kathak (b) Manipuri
    (c) Bharatnatyam (d) Kuchipudi

24. Which among the following classical musicians is not a *tabla* player?
    (a) Alla Rakha Khan (b) Kishan Maharaj
    (c) Nikhil Ghosh (d) Pannalal Ghosh

25. Which musical instrument does Amjad Ali Khan play?
    (a) Sitar (b) Sarod
    (c) Veena (d) Vichitra Veena

26. Which musical instrument did Bismillah Khan Ali excell in?
    (a) Shehnai (b) Santoor
    (c) Sitar (d) Veena

27. Which among the following classical musicians did not receive the Bharat Ratna?
    (a) M.S. Subbalakshmi (b) Kumar Gandharva
    (c) Pandit Ravi Shankar (d) Bade Ghulam Ali Khan

28. What is the term for the ritual hand gestures in Hindu religious dancing?
    (a) Dhyan (b) Mudra
    (c) Jnan (d) Varada

29. In which Indian state are these dances most popular: Panthi, Raut Nacha and Soowa?
    (a) Rajasthan (b) Madhya Pradesh
    (c) Uttarakhand (d) Chhatisgarh

30. Which among the following festivals is not peculiar to Rajasthan?
    (a) Teej (b) Pola
    (c) Gangaur (d) Phulera Dooj

WORLD ART AND CULTURE

1. Who created the *Mona Lisa*, famous for her mysterious smile, which is also regarded as the most famous painting in the history of art?
   (a)Andrea Mantegna (b) Tomasso Masaccio
   (c) Michelangelo (d) Leonardo da Vinci

2. Which among the following paintings in the form of a mural on the wall in the dining hall of the Convent of Santa Maria delle Grazie in Milan was Leonardo da Vinci's creation?
   (a) The Colossus (b) The Last Supper
   (c) Medonna and Child (d) Birth of Venus

3. Which famous Russian artist and a philosopher settled in India established the International Institute of the Himalayan studies and was the father-in-law of the famous Indian actress Devika Rani?
   (a) Lev Russov (b) Nicholas Roerich
   (c) Nikolay Anokhin (d) Fyodor Rokotov

4. Considered by some art critics as the father of Modern Art, who was the official painter of King Charles III? He later became deaf.
   (a) Francisco De Goya (b) Jacques David
   (c)William Blake (d) Paul Gauguin

5. Where can one see Michelangelo's masterpiece paintings in the ceiling of the Sistine Chapel?
   (a) Milan (b) Venice
   (c) Rome (d) The Vatican City

6. Regarded as a leader of the Italian Renaissance, who was the creator of the famous paintings like *The Crucified Christ* with *Virgin Mary, Madonna dell Granduca*, and the *Marriage of the Virgin?*
   (a) Raphael (b) Jacopo Tintoretto
   (c) Paul Ruben (d) Dante Gabriel Rossetti

7. A boyhood friend of famous French novelist Emile Zola and one of the pioneers of new artistic style Cubism, who created the famous painting *The Card Players?*
   (a) Edgar Degas (b) Paul Cezanne
   (c) Camille Pissaro (d) Eduard Manet

8. This 'poor' painter lived for 'art for art's sake' and created hundreds of paintings including his masterpiece *The Starry Night*. Name this Dutch painter who spent his later life in a mental asylum, and died at 39, two years after attempting to kill himself?
   (a) Antony van Dyke (b) Francisco De Goya
   (c) Vincent van Gogh (d) Rembrandt Van Rijn

9. Which among the following pieces of art is not the creation of Michelengelo, one of the most important artists of the Renaissance?
   (a) *Pieta* (b) *The Last Judgement*
   (c) *David* (d) THE SWINEHERD

10. What was the nationality of Rembrandt Van Rijn, considered one of the greatest painters in the world?
    (a) German (b) Dutch
    (c) Italian (d) Spanish

11. Can you reveal the polpular short name by filling in the two empty spaces – one in the beginning and the other at the end of his full name — _____ Diego Jose Francisco de Paula Juan Nepomuceno Maria de los Remedios Cipriano de la Santisima Trinidad Clito Ruiz ____. He was among the greatest painters who created more than 20,000 works of art.
    (a) Paul Signac (b) Amedeo Modigliani
    (c) Pablo Picasso (d) Salvador Dali

12. To which country did Francisco Jose de Goya y Lucientes belong?
    (a) Portugal (b) Spain
    (c) Holland (d) Austria

13. What was the nationality of Rembrandt, one of the greatest painters of all time?
    (a) Swiss (b) Dutch
    (c) Spanish (d) Italian

14. Which constructed international auxiliary language was created by a Polish ophthalmologist and philologist join name L.L. Zamenhof in 1887?
    (a) Volapuk (b) Universalglot
    (c) Mundolinco (d) Esperanto

15. On which date is the World Day for Cultural Diversity for Dialogue and Development celebrated every year, as declared by the UNESCO?
    (a) 21 March (b) 21 April
    (c) 21 May (d) 21 June

16. Who was the rock star and drummer for the Beatles?
    (a) John Lennon (b) George Harrison
    (c) Ringo Starr (d) Paul McCartney

17. Which city in India did Beatles visit in February 1968 to attend an advanced Transcendental Meditation (TM) training session at the ashram of Maharishi Mahesh Yogi?
    (a) Rishikesh (b) Pune
    (c) Varanasi (d) Puri

18. Among the Beatles, who was married to Yoko Ono, Japanese artist and peace activist?
    (a) John Lennon (b) George Harrison
    (c) Ringo Starr (d) Paul McCartney

19. Which resort city on the French Riviera is the site of a famous annual film festival?
    (a) Nice (b) Locarno
    (c) Cannes (d) Karlovy Vary

20. What was the nationality of Wolfgang Amadeus Mozart, one of the greatest composers in the history of Western music?
    (a) Austrian (b) German
    (c) Swiss (d) Portuguese

21. Which is the most prestigious award given out at The Cannes Film Festival for the best films?
    (a) Grand Prix (b) Prix Vulcain
    (c) Palme d'Or (d) Caméra d'Or

22. Who directed the movie *2001: A Space Odyssey*?
    (a) Steve McQueen (b) Ingmar Bergman
    (c) Stanley Kubrick (d) Alfred Hitchcock

23. Where is the Karlovy Vary International Film Festival held?
    (a) Croatia (b) Poland
    (c) Bulgaria (d) Czech Republic

24. Which actress won the Best Actress Academy Award for her leading role in the movie *Roman Holiday?*
    (a) Julie Christie (b) Angelina Jolie
    (c) Jane Fonda (d) Audrey Hepburn

25. Who was the first black to win an Academy Award for Best Actor for his role in *Lilies of the Field?*
    (a) Will Smith (b) Denzel Washington
    (c) Sidney Poitier (d) Paul Winfield

26. Who was the director of the award-winning movie *Avatar*?
    (a) Martin Scorsese (b) Alexander Payne
    (c) James Cameron (d) Woody Allen

27. Ang Lee directed this film, which was perceived as one of the best movies of 2012, and also bagged four Oscars?
    (a) Lincoln (b) The Tree of Life
    (c) The Skin I Live in (d) Life of Pi

28. The largest film festival in the African continent is the Panafrican Film and Television Festival of Ouagadougou. In which African country is it organised?
    (a) Liberia (b) Botswana
    (c) Ivory Coast (d) Burkina Faso

29. Which of the following awards is given to recognize outstanding achievement in music?
    (a) Tony Award (b) Goya Award
    (c) Grammy Award (d) Emmy Award

30. Who directed the film *E.T.: The Extra Terrestrial*?
    (a) Frank Kapra (b) John Ford
    (c) Steven Spielberg (d) Stanley Kubrick

INDIAN LITERATURE

ଔ

1. Which 13th century Sufi poet from Delhi created Qawwali on the lines of *bhajans*?
   (a) Amir Khusro
   (b) Sheikh Farid
   (c) Wali Muhammad Wali
   (d) Muhammad Quli Qutub Shah

2. Which 15th century poet and musician wrote "*Prabhu more avagun chitta na dharo....*"?
   (a) Mirabai (b) Raskhan
   (c) Surdas (d) Tulsidas

3. Who is officially recognised as the national poet of Bangladesh?
   (a) Syed Shamsul Huq (b) Hasan Hafizur Rahman
   (c) Farrukh Ahmed (d) Kazi Nazrul Islam

4. What was the pen-name of Asadullah Baig Khan, one of the greatest poets in Urdu language?
   (a) Zauk (b) Dard
   (c) Ghalib (d) Mir

5. Who is regarded as the 'father of Hindi literature'?
   (a) Mahavir Prasad Dwivedi
   (b) Kamta Prasad Guru
   (c) Devaki Nandan Khatri
   (d) Bharatendu Harishchandra

6. Who penned *Durgeshnandini,* the first Bengali romantic novel published in 1865?
   (a) Sarat Chandra Chatterji
   (b) Bibhutibhushan Bandopadhyay
   (c) Tarashankar Bandopadhyay
   (d) Bankim Chandra Chatterjee

7. Which is the most prestigious literary award in India?
   (a) Kamal Kumari National Award
   (b) Saraswati Samman
   (c) Sahitya Akadami Puruskar
   (d) Bhartiya Jnanpith Award

8. Which prominent Urdu poet wrote "*Saare jahan se achchha...*"?
   (a) Raja Mehdi Ali Khan (b) Naresh Kumar Shad
   (c) Faiz Ahmed Faiz (d) Muhammad Iqbal

9. Which Gujarati author, who is well-known for penning *Jeevan Ek Natak,* won the Jnanpith Award in 1985?
   (a) Mahadev Desai (b) Pannalal Patel
   (c) Narsinh Mehta (d) Ramanbhai Nilkanth

10. What was the real name of Sahir Ludhianvi, a popular Urdu poet and lyricist?
    (a) Hasan Askari (b) Ahmad Bashir
    (c) Abdul Hayi (d) Faruqi Nisar Ahmed

11. Which of the following books is written by Vijay Tendulkar?
    (a) *Kayar* (b) *Charandas Chor*
    (c) *Dipshikha* (d) *Ghashiram Kotwal*

12. Who is the author of *The Flight of Pigeons*?
    (a) Ruskin Bond (b) Vikram Seth
    (c) Rohinton Mistry (d) Shobha De

13. Which Indian writer in English has received a Sahitya Akademi Award in 1978 for her novel *Fire on the Mountain*?
    (a) Kiran Desai (b) Anita Mazumdar Desai
    (c) Shobha De (d) Arundhati Roy

14. Which famous Hindi poet wrote books like *Ansu*, *Lahar,* and *Kamayani* ?
    (a) Sumitranandan Pant
    (b) Maithili Sharan Gupt
    (c) Jaishankar Prasad
    (d) Subhadra Kumari Chauhan

15. Munshi Premchand is regarded as one of the greatest short story writers and novelists in the Indian subcontinent and has to his credit dozens of novels and over 250 short stories. What was his real name?
    (a) Ganpat Rai (b) Dhanpat Rai
    (c) Amrit Rai (d) Lajpat Rai

16. He wrote in Hindi and is regarded as the National Poet. His portrait was unveiled in the Central Hall of the Parliament of India by Prime Minister Dr. Manmohan Singh on the occasion of his centenary year in 2008?
    (a) Nagarjun
    (b) Gajanan Madhav Muktibodh
    (c) Ramdhari Singh 'Dinkar'
    (d) Sachchidananda Vatsyayan

17. Who among the following Hindi writers is famous for writing historical novels?
    (a) Rangeya Raghav (b) Vrindavan Lal Verma
    (c) Kedarnath Agarwal (d) Rajinder Singh Bedi

18. Instituted in 1961, Jnanpith Award is the most prestigious literary honour in the country. Trust of which business family founded this award?
    (a) Sahu Jain family (b) Birla family
    (c) Kirloskar family (d) Bajaj family

19. Who was the first awardee of the prestigious Jnanpith Award in 1965?
    (a) G. Sankara Kurup (b) Tarasankar Bandyopadhyay
    (c) Umashankar Joshi (d) Sumitranandan Pant

20. What is the pen name of Gaura Pant who wrote fictions like *Shamshan Champa, Chal Khusaro Ghar Aapne, Chaudah Phere*, and many others?
    (a) Bhawani (b) Mrignayani
    (c) Shivani (d) Ragini

21. Which famous poet has written *Gul-e-Naghma* in Urdu and received the Jnanpith Award in 1969?
    (a) Qurratulain Hyder (b) Hasrat Jaipuri
    (c) Firaq Gorakhpuri (d) Majrooh Sultanpuri

22. Who among the following writers has not written in Kannada?
    (a) K. Shivaram Karanth
    (b) Masti Venkatesha Iyengar
    (c) Vinayaka Krishna Gokak
    (d) Viswanatha Satyanarayana

23. Name the winner of the coveted Padma Bhushan, Punjab Rattan and Padma Vibhushan awards, who has written the well-known novel *Train to Pakistan*?
    (a) Amrita Pritam (b) Mulk Raj Anand
    (c) Kuldip Nasyar (d) Khushwant Singh

24. According to *The New York Times,* which Indian author is the biggest selling English language novelist in India's history?
    - (a) Chetan Bhagat
    - (b) Ruskin Bond
    - (c) Khushwant Singh
    - (d) Jhumpa Lahiri

25. A talented writer, novelist, and a poet, who is best known for his epic novel *A Suitable Boy*?
    - (a) Gita Mehta
    - (b) Deepak Chopra
    - (c) Vikram Seth
    - (d) Vikram Chandra

26. Which lyricist of Bollywood composed the song "*Yeh kaun chitrakar hai...*" sung by Mukesh in the movie *Boond Jo Ban Gayi Moti*?
    - (a) Bharat Vyas
    - (b) Anand Bakshi
    - (c) Gulzar
    - (d) Majrooh Sultanpuri

27. Who among the folloing is the author of *Aag Ka Daria*?
    - (a) Mohan Rakesh
    - (b) Qurratulain Hyder
    - (c) Habib Tanvir
    - (d) Ismat Chugtai

28. Which famous poet composed the song "*Nuktachee Hai Gham-e-dil...*" sung by K.L. Saigal in the film *Yahoodi ki Ladki*?
    - (a) Mirza Ghalib
    - (b) Mir Taqi Mir
    - (c) Pankaj Mullick
    - (d) Sahir Ludhianvi

29. Which Indian American author published his first novel *The Circle of Reason* in 1986 and won the Prix Medici Estranger, one of France's top literary awards?
    - (a) Eunice De Souza
    - (b) Amitav Ghosh
    - (c) Sheila Murphy
    - (d) Deepak Chopra

30. Which prominent Assamese poet and politician became the President of the Assam Sahitya Sabha in 1972 and was regarded as one of the pioneers of modern literary movement in Assam?
    (a) Hem Barua (b) Atul Chandra Hazarika
    (c) Hiren Bhattacharya (d) Homen Borgohain

WORLD LITERATURE

1. Which Anglo-Irish satirist and essayist is well-known for his *Gulliver's Travels*?
   (a) Oscar Wilde (b) James Joyce
   (c) Jonathan Swift (d) Oliver Goldsmith

2. Which poet, one of the greatest British of English Romantics, died at the age of 36? His daughter Augusta Ada collaborated with Charles Babbage to work on the analytical engine.
   (a) William Blake (b) Lord Byron
   (c) John Keats (d) Robert Browning

3. What was the pen-name of American author Samuel Langhorne Clemens?
   (a) T. H. Lain (b) Voltaire
   (c) Mark Twain (d) N.W. Clerk

4. Which famous novel was written by the Irish author James Joyce?
   (a) *Ulysses* (b) *Lolita*
   (c) *Jaws* (d) *Gone with the Wind*

5. Which Nobel Prize-winning American author is most famous for his *A Farewell to Arms*?
   (a) Stephen King (b) Erle Stanley Gardner
   (c) Dominic Mance (d) Earnest Hemingway

6. 'Saki' is the pen-name of which British short story writer?
   (a) Ben Jonson (b) H.H. Munro
   (c) Sir Walter Raleigh (d) Walter de la Mare

7. Name the famous author who refused to receive the Nobel Prize for Literature in 1963?
   (a) Franz Kafka (b) Boris Pasternek
   (c) Jean-Paul Sartre (d) Albert Camus

8. Which Nobel Laureate poet was once Mexican ambassador to India?
   (a) Pablo Neruda (b) Octavio Paz
   (c) Julio Cortazar (d) Manuel Garcia-Carpintero

9. Which is Shakespeare's shortest tragedy?
   (a) *Macbeth* (b) *Othelo*
   (c) *King Lear* (d) *Romeo and Juliet*

10. French novelist Emile Zola is most famous for which novel?
    (a) *La Peste* (b) *The Godfather*
    (c) *Nana* (d) *She*

11. Who wrote Ancient Mariner, name of a character in the poem of the same name who describes his supernatural experiences to wedding guests?
    (a) John Keats (b) William Wordsworth
    (c) George Shelvocke (d) Samuel Coleridge

12. Which cruel money lender in Shakesopeare's *The Merchant of Venice* was bent on taking a pound of flesh from the body of Antonio?
    (a) Bassanio (b) Shylock
    (c) Brutus (d) Gratiano

13. Who was the heroine of Shakespeare's *Much Ado About Nothing*, famous for her witty dialogues?
    (a) Beatrice (b) Cordelia
    (c) Ursula (d) Margaret

14. Who is considered the 'Father of English Literature'?
    (a) Ben Jonson (b) Christopher Marlowe
    (c) Geoffrey Chaucer (d) William Shakespeare

15. In addition to his scientific acumen, which Persian poet is world fmous for his *Rubaiyats*?
    (a) Nizami Ganjavi (b) Imru al Qays ibn Hujir
    (c) Khalil Gibran (d) Omar Khayyam

16. Which English writer, most famous for his *Utopia* was beheaded on 6 July 1935 because he refused to accept the King as the Head of the Church of England?
    (a) Thomas Moore (b) Thomas Campion
    (c) Edond Spenser (d) William Tyndale

17. Where did Miguel Cervantes, one of the greatest Spanish writers, write his most famous work *Don Quixote*?
    (a) In prison (b) During sea travel
    (c) In a small village (d) In Sancho Panza

18. What genre does the great work of Milton, *Paradise Lost*, fall under?
    (a) Drama (b) Novel
    (c) Epic poem (d) Essay

19. Which science fiction writer penned *War of the Worlds,* an interesting novel about the attack of the Martians on Earth?
    (a) Irving Wallace (b) H.G. Wells
    (c) Arthur Hailey (d) Ian Fleming

20. Which famous book was written by Mary Shelley, wife of famous poet Percy Bysshe Shelley, when she was nineteen?
    (a) *The White Devil* (b) *Adonais*
    (c) *Frankenstein* (d) *Treasure Island*

21. Which great English playwright and famous literary figure died at the age of 94 after falling off a ladder?
    (a) Thomas Hardy (b) Somerset Maugham
    (c) Charles Dickens (d) George Bernard Shaw

22. In which field of knowledge did Lewis Carroll excel other than writing for children and specially famous for his masterpiece *Alice's Adventures in Wonderland*?
    (a) Astronomy (b) Mathematics
    (c) Physics (d) Chemistry

23. Mary Ann Evans, author of *The Mill on the Floss* and *Silas Marner* was better known as:
    (a) Emily Bronte (b) Enid Blyton
    (c) George Eliot (d) Madam Bovary

24. What is Alexei Peshkov, who authored *Mother*, popularly known as?
    (a) Maxim Gorky (b) Fyodor Dostoevsky
    (c) Ivan Turgnev (d) Anton Chekhov

25. What was the pen name of William Sydney Poiter?
    (a) Charles Dickens (b) George Orwell
    (c) O Henry (d) Saki

26. Which of the following famous books was not written while the author was in prison?
    (a) *War and Peace* by Leo Tolstoy
    (b) *Pilgrim's Progress* by John Bunyan
    (c) *Hymn to the Pillory* by Daniel Defoe
    (d) *Glimpses on World History* by Jawaharlal Nehru

27. Which fairy-tale writer for children wrote well-known books like *The Early Duckling, The Snow King*, and *The Nightingale*?
    (a) Emile Zola (b) Jonathan Swift
    (c) Honore de Balzac (d) Hans Christian Andersen

28. Though he lived only for 42 years, yet in his short life he created poetries and essays, besides being a journalist, a revolutionary philosopher, and a professor. Who was this national hero of Cuba?
    (a) José Lima (b) José Rivera
    (c) José Donoso (d) José Marti

29. Which Russian Nobel Prize winning writer wrote the famous books *The Gulag Archipelago* and *One Day in the Life of Ivan Denisovich?*
    (a) Alexander Pushkin (b) Alexander Solzhenitsyn
    (c) Ivan Bunin (d) Boris Pasternak

30. Which among the following is not a poem of William Shakespeare?
    (a) *Venus and Adonis* (b) *Much Ado About Nothing*
    (c) *The Rape of Lucrece* (d) *The Passionate Pilgrim*

FAMOUS INDIANS

1. The British called him the 'Father of Indian Unrest', he remained in exile in Burma for six years. Who was this great Indian patriot who once said, " Swaraj is my birthright"?
   (a) Gopal Krishna Gokhale (b) Bal Gangadhar Tilak
   (c) Lala Lajpat Rai (d) D.K. Karve

2. He founded Servants of India Society in 1905. A great statesman whom Gandhiji regarded as his political guru. Who was he?
   (a) Khan Abdul Gaffar Khan (b) Motilal Nehru
   (c) Madan Mohan Malviya (d) Gopal Krishna Gokhale

3. He brought about the abolition of the cruel custom of Sati (burning of the widows on the funeral pyre of her husband), encouraged scientific education, denounced idol worship and caste system, and formed the Brahma Samaj. Who was he?
   (a) Sri Aurbindo Ghosh (b) Keshub Chander Sen
   (c) Devendranath Tagore (d) Raja Ram Mohan Roy

4. Mahatma Gandhi called her "a woman of great spirited beauty". She died at the age of 39 of tuberculosis. When she served a two-month imprisonment, she said on the twenty-sixth day of the sentence, "I am proud to follow in the footsteps of my husband". Who was she?
   (a) Kasturba Gandhi (b) Kamala Nehru
   (c) Swaruprani Nehru (d) Annie Besant

5. Which Christian lady delivered a number of lectures on Hinduism, translated and popularised the *Gita*, and started a Hindu College in Banaras which has now grown into the Banaras Hindu University?
   (a) Mira Ben (b) Sister Nivedita
   (c) Devika Roerich (d) Annie Besant

6. Which Chief Minister of Tamil Nadu formed Dravida Munetra Kazhakam?
   (a) C.N. Annadurai (b) M. G. Ramachandran
   (c) K. Kamraj (d) E.V. Ramaswamy Naicker

7. Margaret Noble was an Irish lady who came to India and became a disciple of Swami Vivekananda. What name did she adopt for herself after that?
   (a) Sister Nivedita (b) Mira Ben
   (c) Mahishi Devi (d) Rukmani Devi

8. Who founded the Santiniketan Ashram, which later developed to become the Visva-Bharati University?
   (a) Satyendranath Bose (b) Dwarkanath Tagore
   (c) Rabindranath Tagore (d) Debendranath Tagore

9. Recipient of many awards, he is best known for his work on leprosy patients. The name of this famous social activist is 'Murlidhar Devidas', but he is popularly known as:
   (a) Vaman Kane (b) Baba Amte
   (c) Dhonde Keshav Karve (d) Vinoba Bhave

10. He was an associate of Mahatma Gandhi and gifted a village to him which Gandhiji named *Sevagram*. Who was this founder of Satyagraha Ashram at Wardha?
    (a) G.D. Birla (b) Jamnalal Bajaj
    (c) K.M. Munshi (d) K.M. Panikkar

11. She is a great emancipator of women in the self-employment sector. She did tremendous work in trade union of poor women. She was awarded Magsaysay award in 1977. Who is she?
    (a) Kumkum Das (b) Damyanti Joshi
    (c) Medha Patkar (d) Ela Bhatt

12. Who coined the phrase, "unity in diversity" to describe the country?
    (a) Jawaharlal Nehru (b) Mahatma Gandhi
    (c) Mother Teresa (d) Sardar Ballabh Bhai Patel

13. Who was this Vedic scholar and freedom fighter who was awarded Bharat Ratna in 1955?
    (a) Bhagwan Das (b) Purshottam Das Tandon
    (c) Pandurang Vaman Kane (d) Dhondo Keshav Karve

14. She founded Home Rule League in 1916 and was the first woman president of Indian National Congress. Who was this lady to be the President of Theosophical Society of India?
    (a) Madam Kama (b) Annie Besant
    (c) Rani Gaidinliu (d) Sister Nivedita

15. He was the first Indian to become a professor of a college and was elected the President of the Indian National Congress thrice. Who is this great son of India who is also called the 'Grand Old Man of India'?
    (a) Ajmal Khan (b) Sir Surendranath Banerjee
    (c) Rafi Ahmed Kidwai (d) Dadabhai Naoroji

16. Who was the first Education Minister of Independent India?
    (a) Aruna Asaf Ali (b) Maulana Abul Kalam Azad
    (c) S. Srinivasa Iyengar (d) Rajkumari Amrit Kaur

17. Subhas Chandra Bose was elected Congress President twice and also formed a new party, i.e. All India Forward Block. During the World War I, where was he reportedly killed in an air crash on 18 August 1945?
    (a) Tokyo (b) Guam Island
    (c) Taipei (d) Hong Kong

18. Which brilliant scholar and great freedom fighter studied at the Universities of Berkeley, United States and on return to India palayed a crucial role in the Quit India movement?
    (a) Minoo Masani (b) Ram Manohar Lohia
    (c) H. N. Bahuguna (d) Jayaprakash Narayan

19. Where did Mahatma Gandhi coin the term *Satyagrah*?
    (a) Durban (b) Porbandar
    (c) Wardha (d) Dandi

20. What is the popular name of Agnes Gonxha Bojaxhiu, one of India's greatest daughters?
    (a) Annie Besant (b) Mother Mira
    (c) Sister Nivedita (d) Mother Teresa

21. The largest university in the world is named after which Indian? She was also the fourth woman elected president of the Indian National Congress.
    (a) Dr. Zakir Hussain (b) Jawaharlal Nehru
    (c) Indira Gandhi (d) Sir Syed Ahmed Khan

22. Which fact among the following alternatives is not correct about Rabindra Nath Tagore?
    (a) He was awarded the knighthood in 1915
    (b) He started painting at the age of 70
    (c) He never went to any school but studied at home
    (d) His poem '*Amar shonar Bangla*' became the national anthem of Bangladesh

23. Where did Jawaharlal Nehru live during his tenure as Prime Minister?
    (a) Motilal Nehru Road (b) Teen Murti Bhawan
    (c) Ferozeshah Road (d) Race Cource Road

24. In which university did Rajiv Gandhi meet Edvige Antonia Albina Maino (Sonia Gandhi) for the first time and later married her?
    (a) Cambridge University (b) Oxford University
    (c) City University (d) University of London

25. Which ministry was Lal Krishna Adwani holding during the period from May 1977 till July 1979?
    (a) Home (b) Defence
    (c) Industry (d) Information

26. What is the actual name of Anna Hazare, an Indian social activist who led movements to promote rural development and increase government transparency?
    (a) Gajanan Hazare
    (b) Kisan Baburao Hazare
    (c) Vivek Vithal Hazare
    (d) Murlidhar Devidas Hazare

27. Who was the first woman Governor of any state of India?
    (a) Sharada Mukerjee (b) Vijaya Laxshmi Pandit
    (c) Sarojini Naidu (d) Padmaja Naidu

28. Chakravati Rajagopalachari was the first and last Indian Governal General of India. Which Ministry did he hold in Nehru's first cabinet?
    (a) Finance (b) Home
    (c) Defence (d) Education

29. Who was the only President of India to be honoured by the British Knight Bachelor in 1931 and the commonwealth Order of Merit 1963?
    (a) Dr. Rajendra Prasad (b) Dr. S. Radhakrishnan
    (c) Dr. Zakir Hussain (d) Dr. S.D. Sharma

FAMOUS PEOPLE OF THE WORLD

1. Who was the only American president elected to more than two terms (four times)?
   (a) Harry Truman (b) Franklin D. Roosevelt
   (c) Woodrow Wilson (d) James Buchanan

2. At the age of 24, who was the youngest Prime Minister of Britain?
   (a) John Stuart (b) Sir Robert Walpole
   (c) William Pitt (d) George Canning

3. Who was Prime Minister during the British victory over Napoleon at the 1815 Battle of Waterloo?
   (a) Robert Jenkinson
   (b) George Hamilton Gordon
   (c) Benjamin Disraeli
   (d) Harold Wilson

4. Who was the the only American President to be unanimously elected?
   (a) George Washington (b) Benjamin Franklin
   (c) John Adams (d) Thomas Jefferson

5. Who is the only British prime minister to have received the Nobel Prize in Literature?
   (a) David Lloyd George (b) Winston Churchill
   (c) Neville Chamberlain (d) William Gladstone

6. Which U.S. President said, "Ask not what your country can do for you; ask what you can do for your country" at the time of his inauguration as the President?
   (a) Lyndon Baines Johnson (b) Richard Milhous Nixon
   (c) Abraham Lincoln (d) John Fitzgerald Kennedy

7. Who was the first president of the United States to be inaugurated in Washington, D.C.?
   (a) Grover Cleveland (b) Herbert Clark Hoover
   (c) Thomas Jefferson (d) James Madison

8. Who was the Prime Minister of Britain during the Second World War?
   (a) Winston Churchill (b) Stanley Baldwin
   (c) Clement Attlee (d) Sir Anthony Eden

9. Who was the longest-serving Prime Minister of the United Kingdom of the 20th century?
   (a) Harold Wilson (b) Margaret Thatcher
   (c) Harold Macmillan (d) Sir Alec Douglas-Home

10. Spending 27 years in jail, Nelson Mandela, South Africa's first black President, has received more than 250 awards, including Bharat Ratna, in recognition for his anti-apartheid policy. Which, among the following prestigious awards, did he not receive?
    (a) Nobel Prize (b) Lenin Peace Prize
    (c) Fields Medal (d) Nishan-e-Pakistan

11. With whom did Bill Gates, the current chairman of Microsoft, co-founded the world's largest personal-computer software company?
    (a) Craig Mundie (b) Ray Ozzie
    (c) Paul Allen (d) Ric Weiland

12. Barack Hussein Obama's father Barack Hussein Obama, Sr. migrated to the United States of America from which country?
    (a) Uganda (b) Kenya
    (c) Liberia (d) Tanzania

13. Diana Frances Spencer, popularly known as Lady Diana, married Prince of Wales (Charles) on 29 July 1981. After her marriage, which royal title was she not bearing?
    (a) Duchess of Cornwall (b) Baroness of Kent
    (c) Countess of Chester (d) Princess of Wales

14. Which great Russian political figure once said, "No amount of political freedom will satisfy the hungry masses"?
    (a) Vladimir Lenin (b) Josef Stalin
    (c) Nikita Khrushchev (d) Georgy Malenkov

15. Who was the founding father of the People's Republic of China from its establishment in 1949?
    (a) Zhou Enlai (b) Mao Zedong
    (c) Hua Guofeng (d) Zhang Wentian

16. Though born in poverty, she became the wealthiest Afro-American of the 20th century. Who is this woman, regarded as the most influential woman in the world?
    (a) Mary J. Blige (b) Serena Williams
    (c) Oprah Winfrey (d) Folorunsho Alakija

17. Which nationality was Adolf Hitler holding during the First World War when he was wounded and later dercorated for bravery, receiving the Iron Cross First Class?
    (a) German (b) Belgian
    (c) Austrian (d) Swiss

18. With which former President of Egypt did Col. Gamal Abdel Nasser Hussein lead the Egyptian Revolution of 1952 and overthrew the monarchy of Egypt and Sudan, making Egypt a modern state?
    (a) Muhammad Naguib (b) Mahmoud Fawzi
    (c) Anwar Sadat (d) Tahia Kazim

19. Which great philosopher, economist, and revolutionary socialist has written the famous treatise *Das Kapital*, a critical analysis of political economy?
    (a) Max Weber (b) Georg Wilhelm Hegel
    (c) Karl Heinrich Marx (d) Friedrich Engels

20. Which Vietnamese communist revolutionary leader was the Prime Minister and President of North Vietnam for twenty-four years, and was a key figure in the foundation of the Democratic Republic of Vietnam in 1945?
    (a) Truong Chinh (b) Pham Van Dong
    (c) Ho Chi Minh (d) Ton Duc Thang

21. What was the nationality of Ernesto 'Che' Guevara, a physician, an author, a Marxist revolutionary, a guerrilla leader, and a key figure of the Cuban Revolution?
    (a) Bolivian (b) Cuban
    (c) Mexican (d) Argentine

22. Which British monarch had the longest reign?
    (a) Queen Elizabeth I (b) Queen Elizabeth II
    (c) Queen Victoria (d) None of these

23. What is the actual name of Pele, regarded as the best footballer of all time?
    (a) Nélson de Jesus Silva
    (b) Manuel Francisco dos Santos
    (c) Edvaldo Izídio Neto
    (d) Edison Arantes do Nascimento

24. Which former World No. 1 woman tennis player said about Martina Navratilova: "She's the greatest singles, doubles and mixed doubles player who's ever lived"?
    (a) Billie Jean King (b) Margaret Court
    (c) Chris Evert (d) Steffi Graf

25. Who was the first President of Turkey and was instrumental in abolishing the caliphate and make Turkey a modern state?
    (a) Ali Fethi Okyar (b) Ismet Inonu
    (c) Celal Bayar (d) Mustafa Kamal Ataturk

26. Elizabeth Taylor, one of the world's most famous film stars, was married eight times with seven husbands. Name the one whom she martried twice?
    (a) Michael Wilding (b) Richard Burton
    (c) Larry Fortensky (d) Eddie Fisher

27. A fellow of the Royal Society, Bertand Russell was a British philosopher, logician, and mathematician. He was a prominent anti-war activist and an outspoken advocate of nuclear disarmament. In which discipline was he awarded the Nobel Prize in 1950?
    (a) Physics (b) Physiology
    (c) Peace (d) Literature

28. Which great 19th century philosopher, best known for his book *The World as Will and Representation*, was highly influenced by Eastern thought and used to say "truth was recognized by the sages of India"?
    (a) Friedrich Nietzsche (b) Arthur Schopenhauer
    (c) Richard Wagner (d) Ludwig Wittgenstein

29. Which famous neurologist is regarded as the founding father of psychoanalysis?

    (a) Ivan Pavlov (b) Carl Jung

    (c) Sigmund Freud (d) Jean Piaget

30. Which great writer and moral thinker's book *The Kingdom of God is Within You* had a profound impact on Mahatma Gandhi?

    (a) Immanuel Kant (b) Leo Tolstoy

    (c) Bertand Russell (d) Arthur Schopenhauer

FIRST IN INDIA

ᴄʒ

1. Who was the first person of foreign origin to win the Bharat Ratna?
   (a) Mother Teresa (b) Khan Abdul Gaffar Khan
   (c) Dr. Nelson Mandela (d) Dalai Lama

2. Who, among the following was <u>not</u> the first to be awarded the Bharat Ratna in 1954?
   (a) Dr. Bhagwan Das
   (b) Chakravarti Rajagopalachari
   (c) Dr. C.V. Raman
   (d) Dr. Sarvepalli Radhakrishnan

3. Who is the only woman in the world to have climbed the Mt. Everest twice – in May 1992 and May 1993?
   (a) Bachendri Pal (b) Sunita Yadav
   (c) Santosh Yadav (d) Madhu Nautiyal

4. Who was the fist Indian woman to be chosen Miss World?
   (a) Shushmita Sen (b) Rita Faria
   (c) Aishwarya Rai (d) Parsis Khambata

5. Who was the first Indian to be awarded the Pulitzer Award for fiction?
   (a) Arundhati Roy (b) Salman Rushdie
   (c)Vikram Seth (d) Jhumpa Lahiri

6. Who was the first Governor General of Bengal?
   (a) Lord Clive (b) Warren Hastings
   (c) Lord Canning (d) Earl Cornwallis

7. Who was the first Commander-in-Chief of Independent India?
   (a) General Robert Lockhart
   (b) General K. M. Cariappa
   (c) General Archibald Wavell
   (d) General Roy Bucher

8. Who was the first man to climb Mt. Everest without oxygen?
   (a) Phu Dorji (b) Nwang Gombu
   (c) Reinhold Messner (d) Lino Lacedelli

9. Who was the first woman President of Indian National Congress?
   (a) Sarojini Naidu (b) Annie Besant
   (c) Rajkumari Amrit Kaur (d) Vijaya Laxmi Pandit

10. Who was the first woman judge in Supreme Court of India?
    (a) Ranjana Desai (b) Gyan Sudha Mishra
    (c) Leela Seth (d) Meera Sahib Fatima Bibi

11. Who is the first Indian woman cricketer to score a double century in an international match?
    (a) Mithali Raj (b) Jhulan Goswami
    (c) Rumeli Dhar (d) Shantha Rangaswamy

12. Who was the first Director General of Police of a state of India?
    (a) Kiran Bedi (b) Kanchan Bhattacharya
    (c) Meeri Borwankar (d) Letika Saran

13. Who was the only Chief of Army staff who became the Field Marshal?
    (a) General S.M.Srinagesh
    (b) General Maharaj Rajendra Sinhji
    (c) General S.F. Rodrigues
    (d) General S.H.F.J. Manekshaw

14. Who was the first recipient of Param Vir Chakra?
    (a) Major Dhan Singh Thapa
    (b) Lance Naik Karam Singh
    (c) Major Som Nath Sharma
    (d) Major Shaitan Singh

15. T. Usha was the first Indian woman to reach the final of any Olympic event. How is she called by her fans?
    (a) Toofan Express (b) Sprint Queen
    (c) Flying Malayali (d) Payoli Express

16. Who is this first winner of the Dada Saheb Phalke award?
    (a) Sulochana (b) Devika Rani
    (c) Durga Khote (d) Kanandevi

17. Between which two railway stations was the first railway line in India started?
    (a) Mumbai and Pune (b) Pune and Kalyan
    (c) Mumbai and Thane (d) Thane and Kalyan

18. Who was the first Indian woman to become a Minister of State?
    (a) Sarojini Naidu (b) Vijaya Lakshmi Pandit
    (c) Sucheta Kriplani (d) Rajkumari Amrit Kaur

19. Who was the first President of the United States to visit India?
    (a) Richard Nixon (b) John Kennedy
    (c) D.W. Eisenhower (d) Jimmy Carter

20. Who was the first athlete to win the Arjuna Award in 1961?
    (a) Trilok Singh (b) Ajmer Singh
    (c) G.S. Randhawa (d) K.L. Powel

21. Who was the first woman athlete to be awarded the Padma Shri?
    (a) M.D. Valsamma (b) Geeta Zutshi
    (c) P.T.Usha (d) Kamaljit Sandhu

22. Who scored the first Test century in cricket for India?
    (a) Nawab of Pataudi (b) Amar Singh
    (c) Vijay Hazare (d) Lala Amarnath

23. Who is the only Indian batsman to have scored three centuries in his first three Test matches?
    (a) Sunil Gavaskar (b) Cheteshwar Pujara
    (c) Sachin Tendulkar (d) Mohd. Azharuddin

24. Which Indian cricketer has a distinction of taking more wickets (242) than scoring runs (167), a unique world record in cricket history?
    (a) S. Venkataraghavan (b) B.S. Chandrasekhar
    (c) B.S. Bedi (d) E.A.S. Prasanna

25. Who is the only Indian to have scored a century (124) and a double century (220) in a Test match?
    (a) K.S. Duleepsinhji (b) S.M. Gavaskar
    (c) M.L. Jaisimha (d) Sachin Tendulkar

26. Who, in 1951 Delhi Asiad was the fist Indian to win a gold medal in swimming?
    (a) K.P. Thakkar (b) Sachin Nag
    (c) Sebastian Xavier (d) Rima Dutta

27. Who was the first Indian to reach the quarter-final stage of the Wimbledon Championship in 1939?
    (a) S.M. Jacob (b) Sardar Nihal Singh
    (c) Dilip Bose (d) Ghaus Mohammad Khan

28. Who is the only Indian to have reached up to the semi-final stage in Singles of Wimbledon for two consecutive years?
    (a) Ramnathan Krishnan (b) Vijay Amritraj
    (c) Ramesh Krishnan (d) Ramesh Krishnan

29. Which was the first Hindi film to be shown in the United Nations?
    (a) *Kaagaz Ke Phoo*l (b) *Bees Saal Baad*
    (c) *Mother India* (d) *Lage Raho Munna Bhai*

30. Who was the first Indian to get a US patent in 1904?
    (a) Meghnad Saha (b) Jagdish Chandra Bose
    (c) Sir M. Visvesvaraya (d) Ganapathi Thanikaimoni

FIRST IN THE WORLD

1. Which physicist was the first to measure the speed of light successfully without using astronomical calculations?
   (a) Olaf Roemer (b) James Bradley
   (c) Leon Foucault (d) Armand Fizeau

2. Which Italian physicist was the inventor of the first barometer, and was the first to create vacuum over a liquid?
   (a) Gasparo Berti (b) Evangelista Torricelli
   (c) René Descartes (d) Giovanni Battista Baliani

3. Which Dutch naturalist was the first to make a simple microscope and observe protozoa in ponds and bacteria in human mouth?
   (a) Salvino D'Armate (b) Zaccharias Janssen
   (c) Robert Hooke (d) Antonie van Leeuwenhock

4. Who was the first doctor to introduce and study the smallpox vaccine?
   (a) Edward Jenner (b) Charles Maitland
   (c) Emanuel Timoni (d) Dr. Zabdiel Boylston

5. Which South African surgeon performed the first human heart transplant on 3 December 1967 by transferring the heart of a twenty-five-year-old woman into Louis Washkansky, a fifty-five-year-old grocer?
   (a) Alexis Carrel (b) Dickinson Richards
   (c) Andre Cournaud (d) Christian Barnard

6. Who were the first to inject the first inoculation for rabies of a human being on 6 July 1885?
   (a) Dr. George Beran and Emile Roux
   (b) Louis Pasteur and Emile Roux
   (c) Louis Pasteur and Dr. George Beran
   (d) Dr. George Beran, Louis Pasteur and Emile Roux

7. Who was the world's first test-tube baby, born on 25th July 1978 at Oldham General Hospital, Lancashire, England by a team of doctors including Patrick Steptoe?
   (a) Courtney Cross (b) Alastair MacDonald
   (c) Louise Brown (d) Candice Reed

8. Which was the first country in the world to use the birth control pill legally on 9 May 1960?
   (a) United States (b) Britain
   (c) China (d) India

9. Who was the first President of the Chinese Republic?
   (a) Chiang Kai Sheik (b) Chou En Lie
   (c) Mao-Tse-Tung (d) Sun Yat-Sen

10. Who was the first foreign invader to India?
    (a) Sabuktigin Ghazni (b) Muhammad Ghori
    (c) Alexander the Great (d) Mahmud of Ghazni

11. Who was the first person to reach North Pole?
    (a) Roald Amundsen (b) Robert Peary
    (c) Robert Falcon Scott (d) Charles Francis Hall

12. Who was the first woman to scale the Mt. Everest?
    (a) Lakpa Sherpa (b) Bachendri Pal
    (c) Junko Taibei (d) Santosh Yadav

13. Who was the first person to walk in space, officially called the Extra-vehicular activity (EVA) on 18 March 1965?
    (a) Alexei Leonov (b) Mikhail Tyurin
    (c) Edward White (d) F. Story Musgrave

14. Who was the first American woman to go in space in 1983?
    (a) Anna Fisher (b) Kathryn Sullivan
    (c) Sally Ride (d) Kathy Thornton

15. Who was the first woman Prime Minister of a country?
    (a) Chang Sang (b) Maria Estela Peron
    (c) Indira Gandhi (d) Srimavo Bhandarnaike

16. Who is the first Muslim woman to get the Nobel Prize in 2003?
    (a) Zubeida Khan (b) Shirin Ebadi
    (c) Tawakel Karman (d) Ellen Johnson Sirleaf

17. Who, on 24 October 1836, was issued the first US patent for the first friction safety matches, with a mixture of phosphorus?
    (a) Carl Lundstrom (b) Alonzo Dwight Phillips
    (c) Joshua Pusey (d) John Walker

18. Which scientist, on 11 November 1856, was issued the first patent for the manufacture of iron and steel?
    (a) Henry Gilchrist (b) Martin Siemens
    (c) Henry Bessemer (d) Edward Thomas

19. Who, on 23 November 1948, was issued the first US patent for the zoom lens?
    (a) Frank Back (b) Howell Cooke
    (c) Clile C. Allen (d) Roger Cuvillier

20. Which patent was first issued on 25 November 1975 to Robert S. Ledley for the process of using computers to generate a three-dimensional image of the inside of the body?
    (a) Positron Emission Tomography (PET)
    (b) Magnetic Resonance Imaging (MRI)
    (c) Echocardiography
    (d) Computed Axial Tomography (CAT)

21. Who patented the first motorcycle on 29 August 1885?
    (a) Kirkpatrick MacMillan (b) Steve Lucas
    (c) Gottlieb Daimler (d) Hezekiah Bradley Smith

22. Who was the first chess champion in the world?
    (a) Wilhelm Steinitz (b) Emanuel Lasker
    (c) Alexander Alekhine (d) Jose Raul Capablanca

23. Who was the first Prime Minister of Britain?
    (a) Robert Walpole (b) Spencer Compton
    (c) John Stuart (d) Robert Peel

24. Who was the first woman to win an Olympic Gold Medal?
    (a) Betty Robinson (b) Charlotte Cooper
    (c) Marjorie Jackson (d) Suzanne Lenglen

25. What was the speed of the first and only supersonic airliner *Concorde*?
    (a) 2 Mach (b) 2.5 Mach
    (c) 3 Mach (d) 3.5 Mach

26. Who was the first European explorer to reach China?
    (a) Ferdinand Magellan (b) Afonso de Albuquerque
    (c) Marco Polo (d) Jorge Álvares

27. Name the first manned space vehicle sent into space in 1961?
    - (a) Sputnik 1
    - (b) Meriner-1
    - (c) Vostok 1
    - (d) Surveyor 1

28. Which was the first country to win the football World Cup?
    - (a) Italy
    - (b) Uruguay
    - (c) Brazil
    - (d) Chile

29. What was the code name of the first Atom Bomb that was dropped over Hiroshima by the US during the Second World War on 6 August 1945?
    - (a) Fat Boy
    - (b) Little Boy
    - (c) Fat Man
    - (d) Fat Woman

30. Who was the first person to swim across the English Channel?
    - (a) Henry Sullivan
    - (b) Charles Toth
    - (c) Jon Erikson
    - (d) Matthew Webb

ENVIRONMENT

ᏣᏕ

1. Which Indian plant geneticist has been dubbed by the UN as "the Father of Economic Ecology" and as "a living legend who will go into the annals of history as a world scientist of rare distinction"?
   (a) Dr. B.P. Pal (b) Dr. A.B. Joshi
   (c) Dr. H.K. Jain (d) M.S. Swaminathan

2. A conference was held in Stockholm on 5 June 1972 on Human Environment in which it was decided to celebrate World Environment Day every year. On which date is it celebrated throughout the world now?
   (a) 5 May (b) 15 May
   (c) 5 June (d) 15 June

3. How do we refer to a layer of air pollution – discovered in 1999 by Veerabhadran Ramanathan, the Indian atmospheric scientist – that covers parts of the northern Indian Ocean, India, Pakistan, and parts of South Asia, Southeast Asia, and China?
   (a) The Black Cloud (b) The Asian Brown Cloud
   (c) Polluted Brown Cloud (d) Continental Brown Cloud

4. Which 19th century Irish physicist, inventor of a ratio spectrophotometer, was one of the first scientists to recognise the earth's natural greenhouse effect?
   (a) John Tyndall (b) Charles Darwin
   (c) Hollert, Henner (d) Philippe Garrigues

5. He was against the building of Tehri dam, but is best known for the Chipko Movement in Uttarakhand. Who is he?
   (a) Chandi Prasad Bhatt (b) Sunderlal Bahuguna
   (c) Kamla Ram Nautiyal (d) Dev Bahadur Singh

6. In order to create awareness of conserving the habitats of the animal kingdom, in the first week of which month every year do we observe Wildlife Week?
   (a) August (b) September
   (c) October (d) November

7. What is the percentage of nitrogen in the atmosphere by volume?
   (a) 58% (b) 68%
   (c) 78% (d) 88%

8. What does plant and animal kingdom comprise?
   (a) Biosphere (b) Ecosphere
   (c) Aerosphere (d) Centrosphere

9. What is the study of how organisms interact with each other and also with the environment called?
   (a) Edaphology (b) Ecology
   (c) Acology (d) Environment Studies

10. Name the hurricane which started as a tropical storm in the third week of August (2011) and then hit New York and adjoining areas and produced heavy damage to the tune of about three hundred million dollars, one of the costliest in the history of New York?
    (a) Hurricane Katrina (b) Hurricane Hanna
    (c) Hurricane Agnes (d) Hurricane Irene

11. Which word means "the living together in more or less intimate association or close union of two dissimilar organisms"?
    (a) Symbiosis (b) Synergy
    (c) Mutualism (d) Synergism

12. Which phenomenon causes the earth's atmospheric temperature to rise, causing extensive environmental changes?
    (a) Thermal effect (b) Biothermal effect
    (c) Geothermal effect (d) Greenhouse effect

13. Which ecological experiment – initiated on 6 March 1994, contained in a sealed glass and steel structure on a 3.15 acre land at Oracle in Arizona, USA – was meant to explore the possible use of closed biospheres in space colonization?
    (a) Biosphere 1 (b) Biosphere 2
    (c) Biome 1 (d) Biome 2

14. Which chemicals are responsible for depleting the ozone layer?
    (a) Carbon dioxide (b) Sulphur dioxide
    (c) CFCs (d) Nitrogen Oxide

15. *El Niño* is an important temperature fluctuation in surface waters of the tropical Eastern Pacific Ocean. What is the literal meaning of *El Niño*, a Spanish word?
    (a) The big boy (b) The big girl
    (c) The little boy (d) The little girl

16. Which among the following is responsible for contributing roughly 60% of all carbon monoxide emissions worldwide and up to 95% in cities?
    (a) Burning of fossils (b) Industrial units
    (c) Power plants (d) Vehicle exhaust

17. Which greenhouse gas is the main pollutant that is warming Earth?
    (a) Methane (b) Carbon dioxide
    (c) Sulfur dioxide (d) Chlorofluorocarbons

18. Which toxic gas's leakage on 3 December 1984 from the Union Carbide Corporation plant killed more than 4000 people in Bhopal, Madhy Pradesh?
    (a) Methyl isocyanate gas (b) Ethyl isocynate gas
    (c) Hydrogen cyanide (d) Sulfur tetrafluoride

19. Which of the following causes least pollution on Earth?
    (a) Fossil fuels (b) Geothermal energy
    (c) Solar energy (d) Nuclear fission

20. Who coined the phrase "survival of the fittest"?
    (a) Erasmus Darwin (b) Charles Darwin
    (c) Julien Huxley (d) Herbert Spencer

21. With which international agency has India entered into an agreement in 2012 for a project to clean river Ganga with an estimated cost of Rs. 4600 crores?
    (a) World Bank
    (b) Asian Development Fund
    (c) International Monetary Fund
    (d) World Health Organization

22. Which among the following regions in India is the most seismically active places in the world?
    (a) Aravalli (b) Vindhya
    (c) Sheshadri Hills (d) The Himalaya

23. Which environmental disaster, one of the most fierce, ocurred on 26 April 1986 and created danger to the atmosphere?
    (a) Spill of oil on Blight Reef from the oil tanker *Exxon Valdez*
    (b) Explosion in the Fokushima Nuclear Plant
    (c) Explosion in the Chernobyl Power Plant
    (d) Gas leak in the Union Carbide Plant in Bhopal

24. What is termed as the ratio of light from the Sun that is reflected by the Earth's surface, to the light received by it?
    (a) Backflow (b) Albedo
    (c) Boreal (d) Emissions

25. Which Indian state has named its tourist spots on birds?
    (a) Kerala (b) Orissa
    (c) Himachal Pradesh (d) Haryana

26. Which among the following is the main greenhouse gas?
    (a) Oxygen (b) Nitrogen
    (c) Carbon dioxide (d) Sulphur dioxide

27. Established in 1936, which was the first National Park in India, famous for tigers?
    (a) Kanha National Park (b) Sunderbans National Park
    (c) Sariska Tiger Reserve (d) Corbett National Park

28. Among the most threatened animals in the world, which one is chosen as the logo of the World Wildlife Fund when it was established in 1961?
    (a) Polar bear (b) Arctic wolf
    (c) Aardvark (d) Giant panda

29. When on Boxing Day occurred one of the worst natural disasters in recorded history that hits south-eastern Asia when the massive 9.3 magnitude earthquake hit the entire Indian Ocean region killing around 1,86,000 people?

    (a) 2003 (b) 2004

    (c) 2005 (d) 2006

30. Who was the first to propose the idea of global warming in 1824?

    (a) Joseph Fourier (b) Svante Arrhenius

    (c) Dr. Tim Barnett (d) Barry Roger

INDIAN STATES

ଓ

1. Name the aboriginal natives of Odisha and Chhota Nagpur?
   (a) Santhals (b) Garos
   (c) Moplas (d) Todas

2. Which language is spoken in Sikkim and parts of Nepal and Bhutan?
   (a) Kokborak (b) Lepcha
   (c) Angami (d) Karbi

3. The festivals like Losar, Reh, Mopin and Dirang are celebrated in which Indian state?
   (a) Madhya Pradesh (b) Himachal Pradesh
   (c) Rajasthan (d) Arunanchal Pradesh

4. In which city of Karnataka is the Gol Gumbaj situated?
   (a) Bidar (b) Gulbarga
   (c) Bijapur (d) Mysore

5. Which is India's Largest museum?
   (a) National Museum, New Delhi
   (b) Salar Jung Museum, Hyderabad
   (c) Teen Murti Bhavan, New Delhi
   (d) The Prince of Wales Museum, Mumbai

6. Mandovi and Zuari are the two main rivers of which Indian state?
   (a) Goa (b) Maharashtra
   (c) Kerala (d) Meghalaya

7. In which Indian state are these passes situated: Tsang Chok La, Muling La, Thaga La, Mana Pass?
   (a) Uttarakhand (b) Jammu & Kashmir
   (c) Arunachal Pradesh (d) Sikkim

8. Built in the 5th century A.D., this 7.20m high Iron Pillar has not shown any sign of rusting since its existence. From which city was it transported to Delhi in the 12th century?
   (a) Agra (b) Mathura
   (c) Jaipur (d) Udaipur

9. Blackbuck is the state animal of three Indian states. Which among the following is an exception?
   (a) Haryana (b) Punjab
   (c) Gujarat (d) Andhra Pradesh

10. Which Indian state does not have the pink rhododendron as its state flower?
    (a) Assam (b) Nagaland
    (c) Sikkim (d) Himachal Pradesh

11. In which Indian state is the Nehru Zoological Park, the biggest zoo in India, situated?
    (a) Maharashtra (b) Andhra Pradesh
    (c) Tamil Nadu (d) Kerala

12. Where can one find the Kaziranga National Park and the Manas National Park?
    (a) Meghalaya (b) Nagaland
    (c) Assam (d) Sikkim

13. Which temple is dedicated to Lord Shiva and enshrines a *shivalinga*?
    (a) Viswanath Temple, Khajuraho (M.P.)
    (b) Virupaksha Temple, Pattadakal (Karnataka)
    (c) Somaskanda Temple, Chennai (Tamil Nadu)
    (d) Kesava Temple, Belur (Karnatka)

14. To mark the birth anniversary of which guru of Sikh faith is 'Guru Purab' celebrated with great fervour?
    (a) Guru Nanak (b) Guru Harkishan
    (c) Guru Gobind Singh (d) Guru Ramdas

15. What is the playing time of our National Anthem "*Jana Gana Mana* ..." written by Ravindranath Tagore?
    (a) 50 seconds (b) 52 seconds
    (c) 54 seconds (d) 56 seconds

16. Which of the following cities of Uttarakhand is not a district?
    (a) Champawat (b) Bageshwar
    (c) Roorkee (d) Haridwar

17. Built by Shah Jahan in 1648 A.D., the famous Red Fort in Delhi is an imposing red sandstone structure. What is the name of its magnificent entrance gate?
    (a) Delhi Gate (b) Ajmeri Gate
    (c) Turkman Gate (d) Lahori Gate

18. Which is the the tallest building in the country with a total height of 254 metres (833 ft) having 60 floors?
    (a) Imperial Towers, Mumbai
    (b) Alhind Burj, Kozhikod
    (c) Choice Paradise, Kochi
    (d) World Trade Center Banglore

19. The cattle fair held in which town of Bihar is the largest in the state?
    - (a) Darbhanga
    - (b) Sitamarhi
    - (c) Purnia
    - (d) Samastipur

20. Built by Mohammad Quli Qutab Shah in 1591 A.D., where is the four-storeyed structure known as Charminar situated ?
    - (a) Junagarh
    - (b) Patna
    - (c) Mysore
    - (d) Hyderabad

21. According to 2011 census of India, which state has the highest percentage of literacy among females?
    - (a) Goa
    - (b) Mizoram
    - (c) Nagaland
    - (d) Kerala

22. Bluejay is the state bird of which Indian state?
    - (a) Odisha
    - (b) Jammu & Kashmir
    - (c) Himachal Pradesh
    - (d) West Bengal

23. In which Indian state are the Sariska Tiger Reserve and Keoladeo Ghana National Park located?
    - (a) Gujarat
    - (b) Rajasthan
    - (c) Bihar
    - (d) Manipur

24. The second atomic bomb was dropped in the Japanese city of Nagasaki on 9 August 1945, so it is celebrated as the Nagasaki Day. Incidentally we Indians also observe 9 August every year as the
    - (a) Quit India Day
    - (b) Indian Air Force Day
    - (c) Navy Day
    - (d) Armed Forces Flag Day

25. Where can one find Serenity and Karaikul beaches?
    - (a) Kerala
    - (b) Chennai
    - (c) Lakhadweep
    - (d) Puducherry

26. Built in 1995 and having a pinnacle height of 323m, which is the tallest structure in India?
    (a) Palais Royale, Mumbai
    (b) Fazilka TV Tower, Punjab
    (c) Mumbai Television Tower, Mumbai
    (d) Rameswaram T. V. Tower, Tamil Nadu

27. Where did Buddha attain enlightenment?
    (a) Kapilavastu (b) Bodh Gaya
    (c) Sarnath (d) Kusinagara

28. In which Indian state can one find the Shivalik Fossil Park, notable for its life-size models of the vertebrates that might have roamed the Sivalik Hills around two million years ago?
    (a) Madhya Pradesh (b) Tamil Nadu
    (c) Andhra Pradesh (d) Himachal Pradesh

29. In which city of Tamil Nadu is the historic Meenakshi Sundareswarar Temple dedicated to Goddess Parvati located?
    (a) Thanjavur (b) Madurai
    (c) Thirupati (d) Chennai

30. At 560 m, which is the highest waterfall in India?
    (a) Barehipani, Mayurbhanj, Orissa
    (b) Kunchikal, Shimoga, Karnataka
    (c) Vajrai, Satarta, Maharashtra
    (d) Langshiang, West Khasi Hills, Meghalaya

NATIONS OF THE WORLD

1. Which is the largest country in Western Europe?
   (a) France (b) England
   (c) Spain (d) Italy

2. Which is the second largest ocean in the world?
   (a) Arctic (b) Antarctic
   (c) Atlantic (d) Indian

3. Naira is the currency of which of the following countries?
   (a) Niger (b) Nigeria
   (c) Nicaragua (d) Nauru

4. Which nation was a centre of West African civilization for more than 4,000 years?
   (a) Niger (b) Niogeria
   (c) Mali (d) Chad

5. Which small island in the central Pacific Ocean has phosphate as the main source of its economy?
   (a) Nauru (b) Tuvalu
   (c) Samoa (d) Tonga

6. Which country in the eastern Pyrenees lies between Spain and France?
   (a) Aruba (b) Comoros
   (c) Andorra (d) Monaco

7. Which part of the United Kingdom was known as Cambria in Roman times?
   (a) Wales (b) Ireland
   (c) Scotland (d) Britain

8. Which is the largest Greek island in the Mediterranean?
   (a) Corfu (b) Cephalonia
   (c) Creter (d) Chios

9. What is the capital of Kosovo?
   (a) Prizren (b) Prestina
   (c) Peja (d) Mitrovica

10. Portuguese is <u>not</u> the official language of which among the following countries?
    (a) Brazil (b) Cape Verde
    (c) Dominican Republic (d) Guinea-Bissau

11. What is the currency of Bhutan?
    (a) Pula (b) Nakfa
    (c) Lari (d) Ngultrum

12. Rufiya is the monetary unit of which country?
    (a) Indonesia (b) Surinam
    (c) Maldives (d) Mauritius

13. Tagalog, Cebuano, Ilocano, and Bisaya are the races of which Asian nation?
    (a) Laos (b) Thailand
    (c) Cambodia (d) Philippines

14. Other than Italian, which language is spoken in the Vatican City?
    (a) Swiss (b) German
    (c) French (d) Romansh

15. Having a depth of 1741m, which is the deepest lake in the world?
    (a) Baikal, Russia
    (b) Tanganyika, Tanzania-Congo
    (c) Titicaca, Bolivia-Peru
    (d) Caspian Sea

16. 1200 km long and having a depth of about 950m, Caspian Sea is the biggest lake in the world. Through which country, out of the following options, is it not bounded?
    (a) Uzbekistan (b) Kazakhstan
    (c) Turkmenistan (d) Iran

17. Which country has maximum (16) territories, colonies, and dependencies under its jurisdiction?
    (a) France (b) Spain
    (c) United Kingdom (d) United States of India

18. Under the jurisdiction of which country do these territories belong: Saint Helena, Ascension and Tristan da Chunha?
    (a) Spain (b) Portugal
    (c) France (d) United Kingdom

19. Which of the following rivers is the longest?
    (a) Yangtze, China (b) Niger, Niger
    (c) Ob, Russia (d) Mekong, Tibet-China

20. Which of the following mountain peaks is not situated solely in Nepal?
    (a) Dhaulagiri
    (b) Annapurna
    (c) Gyachung Kang
    (d) Kanchenjunga

21. Which country is bordered by the greatest number of other countries (14)?
    (a) China only (b) Russia only
    (c) Both China and Russia (d) None of these

22. Which country has the longest coastline (152,100 miles)?
    (a) Australia (b) Canada
    (c) Russia (d) United States of America

23. Having an elevation of 12,087 feet above sea level, La Paz is the world's highest capital city in the world. In which country is it situated?
    (a) Venezuela (b) Colombia
    (c) Equador (d) Bolivia

24. In which state of USA is the Grand Canyon National Park, a major tourist attraction, situated?
    (a) New Jersey (b) Arizona
    (c) Oklahoma (d) Seattle

25 In which Asian country is Buddhist Ruins of Takht-i-Bahi, a world heritage site, located?
    (a) Pakistan (b) Afghanistan
    (c) Malaysia (d) Indonesia

26. Artificial island Palm Jumeirah, Al Maktoum Bridge, and Jebel Ali beach are the tourist attractions of which Gulf country?
    (a) Dubai (b) Muscat
    (c) Oman (d) Bahrain

27. Which city replaced Lagos in 1976 as the new capital of Nigeria?
    (a) Maiduguri (b) Kano
    (c) Abuja (d) Ibadan

28. Name the capital of Venezuela?
    - (a) Bogota
    - (b) Montvideo
    - (c) Quito
    - (d) Caracas

29. Which is the second most populous country after Brazil in South America?
    - (a) Argentina
    - (b) Colombia
    - (c) Chile
    - (d) Peru

30. Somoni is the monetary unit of which Asian country?
    - (a) Tajikistan
    - (b) Turkmenistan
    - (c) Uzbekistan
    - (d) Kyrgyzstan

INDIAN SCIENCE

ꕤ

1. Who, on 19 December 1945, started Tata Institute of Fundamental Research (TIFR), Mumbai, one of the outstanding research centres in India?
   (a) Jamsetji Tata (b) Sir Dorab Tata
   (c) JRD Tata (d) Homi Jehangir Bhabha

2. Which was the first Indian satellite, launched by a soviet rocket on 19 April 1975 from a cosmodrome near Moscow?
   (a) Bhaskara (b) Rohini
   (c) Aryabhata (d) Kalpana-1

3. Who, in 1981, became the first Indian medical scientist to be elected Fellow of the Royal Society?
   (a) Dr. Avtar Singh Paintal (b) Dr. K. Srinath Reddy
   (c) Dr. Pankaj Jay Pasricha (d) Dr. Tejinder Virdee

4. Who led the first Indian expedition on Antarctica which landed on 9 January 1982?
   (a) Dr. Paramjit Singh Sehra
   (b) Col. Jatinder Kumar Bajaj
   (c) Dr. S.D. Gad
   (d) Dr. S.Z. Qasim

5. Which was the first Indian research station in Antarctica?
   (a) Maitri (b) Dakshin Gangotri
   (c) Bharati (d) Dakshin Yamunotri

6. During which International sports event did Doordarshan introduce colour TV in 1982?
   (a) World Cup Hockey (b) World Cup Cricket
   (c) Commonwealth Games (d) Asian Games

7. Which was India's first nuclear-research reactor inaugurated on 20 January 1957 at Trombay?
   (a) CIRUS (b) Apsara
   (c) Dhruva (d) KAMINI

8. Name India's first operational Earth Observation Satellite, launched on 17 March 1988 by a Soviet Launcher *Vostok*?
   (a) IRS-1A (b) RISAT-2
   (c) Bhaskara-2 (d) IMS-1

9. Which is India's first exclusive satellite for educational facilities launched from Satish Dhawan Space Centre, Sriharikota, into a Geosynchronous Transfer Orbit launched on 20 September 2004?
   (a) JASSO (b) Espresso
   (c) EduBird (d) EDUSAT

10. Who was the first doctor to produce a test tube baby in India?
    (a) Dr. T.C. Anand Kumar
    (b) Dr. Subhash Mukhopadhyay
    (c) Dr. Anup Gupta
    (d) Dr. Indira Hinduja

11. Which Indian chemist laid the foundation of chemical industry in India by setting up the Bengal Chemical and Pharmaceutical Works Ltd?
    (a) Dr. K.A. Hamied (b) Prafulla Chandra Ray
    (c) Rajmitra B.D. Amin (d) Purshotamdas Popatlal

12. Near which mountain in Swiss Alps did Air India's Boeing 707 Kanchenjunga crash resulting in the death of Indian nuclear physicist Homi Jehangir Bhabha on 24 January 1966?
    (a) Monte Rosa (b) Mont Blanc
    (c) Dom (d) Mount Elbrus

13. Who was the first Director of the Council of Scientific and Industrial Research (CSIR) in 1940, who held this post till his death on 1 January 1955?
    (a) Samir K. Brahmachari
    (b) M.K. Bhan
    (c) Raghunath A. Mashelkar
    (d) Sir Shanti Swarup Bhatnagar

14. Which Indian physicist laid the foundation of space research in India?
    (a) Prof. Satish Dhawan (b) Prof. U.R. Rao
    (c) Dr. K Kasturirangan (d) Vikram A. Sarabhai

15. Who was the founder of the Indian Statistical Institute (ISI) in 1931?
    (a) Nikhil Ranjan Sen
    (b) Prasanto Chandra Mahalonobis
    (c) Bimal Kumar Roy
    (d) Pramatha Nath Banerji

16. Which Indian botanist, elected Fellow of the Royal Society in 1965, did extensive research on the embryology of flowering plants and is, thus, rightly called the father of modern embryology?
    (a) Birbal Sahni (b) Ganapathi Thanikaimoni
    (c) Triloki Nath Khoshoo (d) Panchanan Maheshwari

17. Which world-renowned Indian ornithologist is considered as the 'Birdman of India'?
    (a) Humayun Abdulali (b) Biswamoy Biswas
    (c) Salim Ali (d) Syed Abdulla Hussain

18. For which disease, the second-largest parasitic killer in the world after malaria, did Upendra Nath Brahmachari discover a drug, saving millions of lives in Bengal and Assam?
    (a) E. coli Infection (b) Gastroenteritis
    (c) Kala Azar (d) Amoebiasis

19. Who became the first Indian elected to the Fellowship of the Royal Society of London in 1837?
    (a) Sir C. V. Raman
    (b) Shanti Swaroop Bhatnagar
    (c) Ardaseer Cursetjee Wadia
    (d) Srinivasa Ramanujan

20. Who assisted Dr C.V. Raman in discovering the Raman Effect?
    (a) K.S. Krishnan (b) Léon Brillouin
    (c) Adolf Smekal (d) L. Mandelstam

21. Which mode of personal identity was used by Sir William Herschel in July 1858 when he was the Chief Magistrate of the Hooghly district in Jungipoor, India?
    (a) Fingerprints (b) Identity Card
    (c) Ration Card (d) Land Ownership Card

22. Elected F.R.S. in 1940, and awarded the Padma Bhushan in 1954 and Bhatnagar Award in1961, who was the first Director of the National Physical Laboratory, New Delhi?
    (a) Prof. M.G.K. Menon (b) Prof. Meghnad Saha
    (c) Prof. P. Maheshwari (d) Dr. K.S. Krishnan

23. Which pilotless target aircraft was introduced in the Indian Air Force on 5 January 2001?
    (a) Parakram (b) Arjuna
    (c) Lakshya (d) Udyesha

24. What day is celebrated on 28 February every year in India?
    (a) Earth Day
    (b) Mother's Day
    (c) National Health Day
    (d) National Science Day

25. The Kalinga prize was instituted for the popularisation of science and presented each year by UNESCO to a person with a distinguished career of service in the interpretation of science and research to the public. Who instituted this prize in 1952?
    (a) Jawahar Lal Nehru
    (b) Homi Jahagir Bhabha
    (c) Biju Patnaik
    (d) Nandini Satpathy

26. What are 'Maitri' and 'Dakshin Gangotri'?
    (a) Two major rivers in India
    (b) Two mountain ranges in western India
    (c) Two western ghats
    (d) Two Indian research stations in Antarctica

27. Which Indian child prodigy was awarded a medical degree at 17 from Mt. Sinai School of Medicine, New York, making him the youngest doctor in the world?
    (a) Akshay Venkatesh
    (b) Priyanshi Somani
    (c) Balamurli Ambat
    (d) Kishan Shrikanth

28. What type of surgery was performed in India on 6 July 1959 for the first time on a twelve-year-old girl by Dr. N. Gopinath and Dr. R.H. Betts at the Christian Medical Hospital, Vellore, Chennai?
    (a) The first open-heart surgery
    (b) The first liver implant
    (c) The first plastic surgery
    (d) The first kidney transplant

29. On 27 October 1998, who performed India's first heart surgery, being assisted by the robot "Aesop 3000" on a sixteen-year-old girl at the Escorts Heart Institute & Research Centre, New Delhi?
    (a) Dr. K.M. Cherian (b) Dr. Venugopal P
    (c) Dr. Devi Prasad Shetty (d) Dr. Naresh Trehan

30. There is much hue and cry about 2G spectrum nowadays, involving top politicians and government officers. It is lebelled the biggest scam in the history of India. What does 'G' in the '2G' stand for?
    (a) Grade (b) Gigabytes
    (c) Global (d) Generation

PHYSICAL SCIENCES

1. Which Swedish scientist, who accurately determined more than 2,000 relative atomic and molecular masses, is considered as a father of modern chemistry?
   (a) William Prout
   (b) Edward Kendall
   (c) Jons Jacob Berzelius
   (d) Nicolas Lablanc

2. Which allotrope of carbon was discovered by Robert F. Curl, Jr., Richard E. Smalley, and Sir Harold W. Kroto, who were awarded the 1996 Nobel Prize for Chemistry for their work?
   (a) Diamond (b) Graphite
   (c) Fullerene (d) Coal

3. Which chemical element number 100 is named after the Italian born American physicist, who directed the first controlled chain reaction involving nuclear fission?
   (a) Meitnerium (b) Fermium
   (c) Bohrium (d) Ruthenium

4. Which material is harder than diamond?
   (a) Tungsten (b) Bessemer steel
   (c) Graphite (d) Borazan

5. Which French scientist in 1802 formulated the law that a gas expands linearly with a constant pressure and rising temperature?
   (a) Robert Boyle (b) Louis-Joseph Gay-Lussac
   (c) Thomas Linacre (d) Sir Humphrey Davy

6. Who, in 1868, discovered helium in the Sun's atmosphere before it had been detected on Earth?
   (a) Norman Lockyer (b) John Wheeler
   (c) Hans Bethe (d) William Hamilton

7. *Ununquadium* and *ununhexium* are the temporary names for the man-made heavy elements with atomic numbers 114 and 116, respectively. Now, what names has the International Union of Pure and Applied Chemistry (IUPAC) proposed for these superheavy elements?
   (a) Flerovium and Livermorium
   (b) Copernicium and Dubnium
   (c) Darmstadtium and Hassium
   (d) Roentgenium and Meitnerium

8. Bose-Einstein condensate is the fifth state of matter after solid, liquid, gas, and plasma. When does it occur?
   (a) At very high temperatures
   (b) When the temperature is at par with the sun
   (c) At temperature below 100 degrees celcius
   (d) At extremely low temperatures

9. Currently, which is the most valuable substance in existence, with an estimated worth of $ 400 billion per milligram because of its difficult production?
   (a) Hafnium nuclear isomers (b) Tantalum nuclear isomers
   (c) Uranium nuclear isomers (d) Antimatter

10. Name the theorem which states, "The total energy of an ideal liquid under streamline flow remains constant"?
    (a) Carnot's theorem (b) Poiseuille's theorem
    (c) Bernoulli's theorem (d) Torricelli's theorem

11. Who propounded the second law of thermodynamics which states that heat can never pass spontaneously from a body at a lower temperature to one at higher temperature?
    (a) Sadi Carnot (b) Rudolph Julius Clausius
    (c) Ludwig Boltzmann (d) Joseph Louis Gay-Lussac

12. Which type of electromagnetic radiation has a wavelength in the range of 10 to 0.01 nanometres, corresponding to frequencies in the range 30 PHz to 30 Ehz?
    (a) Gamma rays (b) X-rays
    (c) U-V rays (d) I-R rays

13. Name the subatomic particles having no detectable mass and no electric charge, and travel with the speed of light?
    (a) Fermions (b) Photons
    (c) Quarks (d) Neutrinos

14. Who discovered the positive electron or positron for which he shared the Nobel Prize in 1936 with Victor Hess?
    (a) Sir James Chadwick (b) Sir George P. Thomson
    (c) Clinton J. Davisson (d) Carl David Anderson

15. Which prestigious award in mathematics did Indian American Sathamangalam Ranga Iyengar Srinivasa Vardhan win in 2007?
    (a) Wolf Prize
    (b) Srinivasa Ramanujan Medal
    (c) Fields Medal
    (d) Abel Prize

16. Which famous astronomer of the eighteenth century discovered infrared radiation?
    (a) Joseph von Fraunhofer (b) Caroline Herschel
    (c) Sir William Herschell (d) Charles Messier

17. Which experiment established the fact that speed of light is constant?
    (a) Davisson–Germer experiment
    (b) Michelson–Morley experiment
    (c) Geiger–Marsden experiment
    (d) Stern–Gerlach experiment

18. Which Scottish physicist proposed that light is a wave and thus formulated the electromagnetic theory?
    (a) Augustin-Jean Fresnel (b) James Clerc Maxwell
    (c) Thomas Young (d) Louis-Victor de Broglie

19. Who was the first to prove that heat and light are electromagnetic radiations?
    (a) Wilhelm von Bezold (b) Heinrich Rudolf Hertz
    (c) James Clerk Maxwell (d) Hermann von Helmholtz

20. Which French physicist was the first to measure the speed of light successfully without using astronomical calculations?
    (a) Armand Hippolyte Fizeau (b) Léon Foucault
    (c) Ole Christensen Romer (d) A.A. Michelson

21. Which Italian physicist and physician discovered that muscle and nerve cells produce electricity, which led to the invention of the voltaic pile, a type of battery?
    (a) Eric R. Kandel (b) Camillo Golgi
    (c) Franz Nissl (d) Luigi Galvani

22. Who was once asked about his greatest contribution to mathematics to which he replied that it was the discovery of Ramanujan?
    (a) Carl G.J. Jacobi
    (b) William R. Hamilton
    (c) Godfrey Harold Hardy
    (d) James J. Sylvester

23. Who was the inventor of the Circular Slide Rule, who also devised a standardised notation for algebra, like ' ::, <>, pi'?
    (a) Johann Bernoulli (b) William Oughtred
    (c) Ernst E. Kummer (d) Pierre-Simon Laplace

24. Which famous mathematician is well known for a series, bearing his name, through which he solved differential equations, and is now used in the analysis of signals in electronics?
    (a) Jean Baptiste Fourier (b) Colin Maclaurin
    (c) Brook Taylor (d) Leonhard Euler

25. Which great Swiss mathematician of the 18th century introduced a number of symbols which are in vogue even today, like Σ for summations, $f(x)$ for a function, π for the ratio of the circumference to the diameter of a circle, etc.?
    (a) Adrien M. Legendre (b) Johann Bernoulli
    (c) Leonhard Euler (d) Gottfried W. Leibniz

26. Which Persian poet, mathematician and astronomer gave a geometric method for solving cubic equations, and also proposed a heliocentric theory before Copernicus gave the explanation?
    (a) Abu Rayhan Biruni
    (b) Alhazen ibn al-Haytham
    (c) Omar Khayyam
    (d) Muhammed al-Khowârizmi

27. Awarded the 1950 Nobel Prize for Literature, which Welsh mathematician, writer and philosopher, published a number of books on theory of logic?
    (a) James J. Sylvester (b) Ferdinand Eisenstein
    (c) Alexis C. Clairaut (d) Bertrand Russell

28. Which French mathematician was the pioneer in the development of analytic trigonometry, and in the theory of probability, besides originating a theorem, bearing his name, which was a link between complex numbers and trigonometry?
    (a) Abraham De Moivre (b) Adrien M. Legendre
    (c) William R. Hamilton (d) Jacob Bernoulli

29. Which Swiss mathematician was the first person to use 'g' to represent the acceleration due to gravity?
    (a) Isaac Newton (b) Siméon-Denis Poisson
    (c) Henri Poincaré (d) Johann Bernoulli

30. Which 'Nobel Prize of Mathematics' is awarded every four years to recognize outstanding mathematical achievement for existing work for the candidate below 40 years of age?
    (a) The Fields Medal (b) Aisenstadt Prize
    (c) Adams Prize (d) Alfréd Rényi Prize

LIFE SCIENCES

1. Which Swedish biologist developed binomial nomenclature to classify and organise plants and animals by 'kingdoms', 'classes', 'orders', 'genera', and 'species'?
   (a) Camillo Golgi (b) Carolus Linnaeus
   (c) Alexis Carrel (d) Karl Ernest von Baer

2. Which greenish-yellow liquid is secreted by the liver?
   (a) Hipaticae (b) Biliverdin
   (c) Bilirubin (d) Bile

3. Which English physician was the first to correctly describe the circulation of blood?
   (a) John Macleod (b) William Harvey
   (c) Edward Wilson (d) Alan Lloyd Hodgkin

4. What are the channels between the uterus and the ovaries called?
   (a) Umbilical cord (b) Follicles
   (c) Fallopian tubes (d) Ureter

5. Who made the first artificial gene?
   (a) Thomas Henry Huxley
   (b) Julius Huxley
   (c) Andrew Fielding Huxley
   (d) Hargobind Khorana

6. Which British physicist and molecular biologist, along with James D. Watson and Maurice Wilkins, was one of the co-discoverers of the structure of the DNA molecule in1953?
   (a) Rachel Carson
   (b) Sir John Carew Eccles
   (c) John Enders
   (d) Francis Harry Compton Crick

7. Which Austrian immunologist and pathologist and winner of the Nobel Prize in 1930, discovered the human blood groups?
   (a) Howard Florey (b) Karl von Frisch
   (c) Karl Landsteiner (d) Thomas Morgan

8. Name the blood cell which protects the body from infection and diseases?
   (a) Haemoglobin (b) Platelets
   (c) White blood corpuscles (d) Red blood corpuscles

9. Which is the largest cell present in the human body?
   (a) Nerve cell (b) Muscle cell
   (c) White blood cell (d) Red blood cell

10. Which Austrian monk and botanist who worked with pea plants laid the foundation of modern genetics?
    (a) Ernest Starling (b) Jean Louis Agassiz
    (c) Joseph Erlanger (d) Gregor Johann Mendel

11. Which branch of science deals with the study of cells and tissues of organisms?
    (a) Histology (b) Historiography
    (c) Historiology (d) Histopathology

12. What is the study of birds called?
    (a) Optology (b) Ornithology
    (c) Orthoepy (d) Orchidology

13. Plants make their food during the process of photosynthesis. In this procoess, oxygen is released in the presence of sunlight by:
    (a) Water (b) Carbohydrates
    (c) Chlorophyll (d) Carbon dioxide

14. Who established the system of classification of the animal kingdom?
    (a) Julien Huxley (b) John Ray
    (c) Carolus Linnaeus (d) Bentham and Hooker

15. Who introduced the term 'cell'?
    (a) Rudolf Virchow (b) Robert Brown
    (c) Robert Koch (d) Robert Hooke

16. Obsession with bees is termed as
    (a) Apimania (b) Entomomania
    (c) Pedomania (d) Ailuromania

17. The irrational fear of heights is termed as
    (a) Agoraphobia (b) Acrophobia
    (c) Ailurophobia (d) Psychrophobia

18. Which branch of science deals with the study of fossils?
    (a) Agronomy (b) Embryology
    (c) Palaeontology (d) Zoology

19. Who was the first to demonstrate the process of photosynthesis?
    (a) William Thomson (b) Gregor Mendel
    (c) Julius Sachs (d) Daniel G. Nocera

20. Ali Maow Maalin was the last recorded victim of small pox. To which country did he belong?
    (a) Somalia (b) Sudan
    (c) Morocco (d) Algeria

21. Which of the following is the white portion of the eye?
    (a) Pupil (b) Iris
    (c) Cornea (d) Sclerotic

22. Which among the following is the largest gland in the human body?
    (a) Liver (b) Brain
    (c) Heart (d) Lung

23. What is the biological name of vitamin H?
    (a) Linoleic acid (b) Folic acid
    (c) Biotin (d) Acetic acid

24. What is the biological name for vitamin M?
    (a) Folic acid (b) Biotin
    (c) Ascorbic acid (d) Acetic acid

25. In which part of the digestive canal does the protein change into peptones?
    (a) Stomach (b) Intestine
    (c) Duodenum (d) Large intestine

26. Which vitamin is necessary for sight and vision?
    (a) Vitamin A (b) Vitamin B12
    (c) Vitamin C (d) Vitamin K

27. Which British pathologist, born in Almora, Uttarakhand, India, discovered the malaria parasite and was awarded the Nobel Prize for Physiology in 1902?
    (a) Carlos Finlay
    (b) Charles Louis Alphonse Laveran
    (c) Sir Patrick Manson
    (d) Sir Ronald Ross

28. Which type of protein produced in the blood or tissues destroys bacteria or neutralizes poisons?
    (a) An antibody (b) Ribozyme
    (c) Amino acids (d) Pathogen

29. What is the smallest living organism in the world?
    (a) Mycoplasma (b) Virus
    (c) Bacteria (d) Prions

30. Excess of which substance – a white sterol present in the tissues of the human body in which it performs a number of important functions – can result in coronary thrombosis in the body?
    (a) Cholesterol (b) Fatty acids
    (c) Triglyceride (d) Sphingolipid

MEDICAL SCIENCES

1. Which international agency of the United Nations is dealing with public health?
   (a) Public Health Foundation (PHF)
   (b) World Federation of Public Health Associations (WFPHA)
   (c) International Committee of the Red Cross
   (d) World Health Organization (WHO)

2. Which British surgeon was the founder of antiseptic surgery?
   (a) Dr. George H. Tichenor
   (b) Louis Pasteur
   (c) Joseph Lister
   (d) Oliver Wendell Holmes, Sr

3. Which was the first antibiotic discovered as a natural product?
   (a) Pyocyanase (b) Penicillin
   (c) Tetracycline (d) Streptomycin

4. English physician Edward Jenner was a pioneer in vaccination. He made a discovery in 1796 that inoculation with cowpox gave immunity to another disease. Name this other ailment?
   (a) Encephalitis (b) Tuberculosis
   (c) Measles (d) Smallpox

5. Who developed the Polio vaccine?
   (a) Maurice Brodie (b) John Kolmer
   (c) Jonas Salk (d) Thomas H. Welle

6. Who isolated TB (Tubercle Bacillus) bacillus on 24 March 1882?
   (a) Dr Richard Morton (b) Albert Calmette
   (c) J.L. Schönlein (d) Robert Koch

7. What is the study of the causes of diseases known as?
   (a) Chiropody (b) Aetiology
   (c) Cytology (d) Epidemiology

8. Which Belgian astronomer, mathematician, statistician and sociologist is famous for his 'Body Mass Index' which remains the official measurement for obesity to this day?
   (a) Andre-Michel Guerry (b) Adolphe Quetelet
   (c) William Estes (d) Martha Berkley Beeler

9. Who, on 14 May 1796, administered the first successful smallpox vaccination inoculated to a young boy named James?
   (a) Viktor Zhdanov (b) Donald Henderson
   (c) Edward Jenner (d) Charles Maitland

10. On 1 September 1865, who performed the first antiseptic surgery?
    (a) Joseph Lister (b) Dr. George H. Tichenor
    (c) Oliver Holmes, Sr. (d) Henry Jacques Garrigues

11. Who, in 1978, was the world's first test-tube baby, born at Oldham General Hospital, Lancashire, England by a team of doctors including Patrick Steptoe?
    (a) Leesa Meldrum (b) Louise Brown
    (c) Kruti Parekh (d) Harsha Chawda

12. Which German physician was the originator of Homeopathy?
    (a) Dr. Constantine Hering
    (b) Dr. Mahendra Lal Sircar
    (c) Dr. James Tyler Kent
    (d) Christian Samuel Hahnemann

13. Which Scottish scientist, a pioneer in the field of family planning, opened Great Britain's first family planning clinic in London?
    (a) Mrs. Audrey Court (b) Dr. Marie Stopes
    (c) Dr. Clara Macirone (d) Dr. Dorothy Sandilands

14. Which nurse opened the first birth control clinic in USA in 1919?
    (a) Dr. Margaret Sanger (b) Dr. Mary Winfield
    (c) Dr. Louise Tyrer (d) Dr. Elizabeth Connell

15. Which French chemist and microbiologist discovered the 'germ theory of disease' – according to which most of the infectious diseases are caused by germs – which became the base for the development of microbiology?
    (a) Robert Koch (b) Louis Pasteur
    (c) Ferdinand Cohn (d) Friedrich Henle

16. Which Italian physician and cytologist discovered the 'neuron' – now named afterr his surname – which led to identification of the neuron as the basic structural unit of the nervous system?
    (a) Camillo Golgi (b) Herbert Boyer
    (c) Walter Gilbert (d) Frank Macfarlane Burnet

17. Which English embryologist led the team of scientists to produce *Dolly*, a Finn Dorset lamb, the first mammal cloned from a cell from an adult at the Roslin Institute, Edinburgh, Scotland on 5 July 1996?
    (a) Keith Campbell (b) Bill Ritchie
    (c) Ian Wilmut (d) Hans Dreisch

18. Who discovered insulin on 15 April 1922?
    (a) Frederick Banting (b) John MacLeod
    (c) Charles Best (d) All the above

19. Which among the following is a reason for women to get extra calcium in food or pills?
    (a) It helps in increasing weight
    (b) It lowers the risk of prostate cancer
    (c) It helps prevent colon cancer
    (d) It lowers the blood sugar level

20. Medical practitioners take the Hippocratic oath. Who takes the Florence Nightingale oath?
    (a) Midwives (b) Lady doctors
    (c) Nannies (d) Nurses

21. What does a sphygnomanometer measure?
    (a)Blood pressure (b) Blood sugar
    (c) Pulse rate (d) Heart beat rate

22. Which substance or hormone causes masculine characteristics?
    (a) Androgyne (b) Androgen
    (c) Androsterone (d) Android

23. Which branch of medical science deals with the study of cancer?
    (a) Physiology (b) Oncology
    (c) Odontology (d) Poleontology

24. Who discovered the different types of bloods?
    (a) Karl Landsteiner (b) Hugo De Vries
    (c) William Harvey (d) Alexander S. Wiener

25. In which part of the digestive canal is protein changed into peptones?
    (a) Stomach (b) Intestine
    (c) Duodenum (d) Large intestine

26. Who were the joint winners of the 2012 Nobel Prize in Physiology or Medicine?
    (a) Sir Johan Gurdon and Shinya Yamanaka
    (b) Bruce Beutler, Jules Haffmann, and Ralph Steinman
    (c) Elizabeth Blackburn, Carol Greider, and Jack Szostak
    (d) Richard Aexl and Linda Buck

27. Who is considered to be the father of immunology?
    (a) Robert Koch (b) Edward Jenner
    (c) Louis Pasteur (d) William Harvey

28. The branch of science concerned with improvement of mankind by applying laws of heredity is termed as:
    (a) Genetics (b) Genetic engineering
    (c) Dysgenics (d) Eugenics

29. Who discovered the red blood corpuscles?
    (a) Robert Hooke (b) Anton van Leeuwenhoek
    (c) Karl Landsteiner (d) William Harvey

30. Who is considered to be the father of modern medicine?
    (a) Aristotle (b) Socrates
    (c) Hippocrates (d) Leeuwenhoek

HEALTH AND NUTRITION

1. Which breakfast cereal did Dr. John Harvey Kellogg invent in 1898?
   (a) Shredded Oats (b) Golden Nuggets
   (c) Crunchy Bran (d) Corn Flakes

2. Having been completely eradicated from the world today, in which African country was the last known case of smallpox reported in October 1977?
   (a) Burundi (b) Niger
   (c) Somalia (d) Mozambique

3. When was the World Vegetarian Day observed for the first time?
   (a) 1 October 1975 (b) 1 October 1976
   (c) 1 October 1977 (d) 1 October 1978

4. Who discovered penicillin?
   (a) Ronald Ross (b) Edward Jenner
   (c) Alexander Fleming (d) None of these

5. Based on ancient Chinese science, Feng Shui is also described as *Dragon Magic* and *Intuitive Living*. What is the literal meaning of Feng Shui?
   (a) Fire and earth (b) Earth and Wind
   (c) Wind and water (d) Water and fire

6. Which trace element is required by the body for several enzymes such as carboxypeptidase, liver alcohol dehydrogenase, and carbonic anhydrase?
   (a) Nickel (b) Manganese
   (c) Zinc (d) Selenium

7. Which among the following is high in iron?
   (a) Orange (b) Lentils
   (c) Egg (d) Carrot

8. Which black solid element giving violet vapours is an essential element in the diet?
   (a) Magnesium (b) Calcium
   (c) Iodine (d) Potassium

9. Goitre and anaemia are caused due to the deficiency of
   (a) Minerals (b) Proteins
   (c) Carbohydrates (d) Vitamins

10. Which day every year is celebrated as Malaria Day?
    (a) 20 June (b) 20 July
    (c) 20 August (d) 20 September

11. Which yoga exercise relaxes the mind and body, eases tension, reduces fatigue and produces a feeling of revitalization?
    (a) Shavasan (b) Tadasan
    (c) Makarasan (d) Padmasan

12. Cancer is:
    (a) Excess cell division
    (b) Reduced cell division
    (c) Excess and uncontrolled cell division
    (d) Reduced cell division with pus formation

13. Which of the following is the factor for African sleeping sickness?
    (a) Musca domestica (b) Tse tse
    (c)) Anafeles (d) Culax

14. Which of the following diseases is spread through water?
    (a) Asthma (b) Tuberculosis
    (c) AIDS (d) Typhoid

15. Which of the following diseases is spread by housefly?
    (a) Malaria (b) Hypertension
    (c) Common cold (d) Typhoid

16. Night blindness is caused due to lack of:
    (a) vitamin A (b) Vitamin B1
    (c) vitamin B2 (d) Vitamin D

17. Which of the following diseases is caused by fungus?
    (a) Cholera (b) Gonorrhea
    (c) Ringworm (d) Typhoid

18. Which of the following diseases is caused due to deficiency of vitamin C?
    (a) Cancer (b) Night blindness
    (c) Malaria (d) Scurvy

19. The disease Beriberi is caused by the deficiency of:
    (a) vitamin A (b) vitamin B1
    (c) vitamin C (d) vitamin E

20. Which among the following is a physiological liver disease?
    (a) Herpes (b) Kala azar
    (c) Influenza (d) Jaundice

21. Which of the following is the richest in protein?
    (a) Sweets (b) Soya bean
    (c) Egg (d) Wheat

22. Which of the following diseases is transmitted by mosquitoes?
    (a) Plague (b) Jaundice
    (c) Filaria (d) Cholera

23. For which of the following is an oral vaccine used?
    (a) Polio (b) Tetanus
    (c) Measles (d) Tuberculosis

24. What was tuberculosis formerly known as?
    (a) White pox (b) White plague
    (c) White vex (d) White pest

25. Linoleic acid is the biological name for:
    (a) Vitamin F (b) Vitamin G
    (c) Vitamin C (d) Vitamin E

26. Name the vitamin whose deficiency leads to the deformation of bones?
    (a) Vitamin D (b) Vitamin C
    (c) Vitamin B (d) Vitamin A

27. Which pneumonia-type disease, also known as SARS, is spreading rapidly from Hong Kong to other parts of Asia?
    (a) Serious Acute Respiratory Syndrome
    (b) Sedate Acute Respiratory Syndrome
    (c) Stringent Acute Respiratory Syndrome
    (d) Severe Acute Respiratory Syndrome

28. On which date every year is the World Health Day observed?
    (a) 7 April (b) 7 May
    (c) 7 June (d) 7 July

29. What international day is observed on 1 December every year?
    (a) World Health Day (b) World AIDS Day
    (c) World Exercize Day (d) World Population Day

30. Which parasitic nematode in the intestine of vertebrates causes anaemia?
    (a) Hookworm (b) Tapeworm
    (c) Vermis (d) Helminth

TRANSPORT AND COMMUNICATION

1. Where on 10 January 1863 was the world's first underground railway inaugurated?
   (a) London (b) Paris
   (c) New York (d) Berlin

2. Introduced on 1 October 1908, which was the first car to be made on an assembly line, produced by Henry Ford's Ford Motor Company at the Piquette Plant in Detroit, Michigan?
   (a) Ford Model A (b) Ford Model T
   (c) Ford Figo (d) Ford Ikon

3. Which Austrian automobile engineer designed the Volkswagen Beetle – meaning 'people's car', a car built for the masses – which was conceptulised by Adolph Hitler?
   (a) Karl Benz (b) Nikolaus Otto
   (c) Ferdinand Porsche (d) Gottlieb Daimler

4. Which German mechanical engineer designed the world's first practical automobile to be powered by an internal-combustion engine in 1885?
   (a) Nicolaus Otto (b) Francois Isaac de Rivaz
   (c) Karl Friedrich Benz (d) Gottlieb Daimler

5. Who designed the first motorcycle?
   (a) Nikolaus Otto
   (b) Pierre Lallement
   (c) Wilhelm Maybach
   (d) Gottlieb Wilhelm Daimler

6. Which double-deck airliner made its first maiden flight on 27 April 2005 from Toulouse, France and commercial flights from Singapore to Sydney on 25 October 2007 with 485 passengers on board?
   (a) Boeing 747 (b) Concorde
   (c) Dornier Do-X (d) Airbus A380

7. Which Air France supersonic airline crashed on 25 July 2000, killing all hundred passengers, nine crew members and four people on ground, while taking off from Charles de Gaulle Airport, after which this airline ceased to operate?
   (a) JAXA's scramjet (b) Airbus A380
   (c) Concorde (d) Tupolev Tu-144

8. Who demonstrated the first electric telegraph at the Speedwell Ironworks near Morristown, New Jersey in January 1838?
   (a) Jean-Antoine Nollet
   (b) Samuel Thomas von Sömmering
   (c) Samuel Morse
   (d) Francisco Salvái Campillo

9. Who is credited for coining the word 'Hello' as a telephone greeting in 1877?
   (a) Thomas Edison
   (b) Alexander Graham Bell
   (c) Mark Twain
   (d) Elisha Gray

10. Other than Alexander Graham Bell, who patented the telephone on the same day, ie. 14 February 1876, but the Supreme Court ruled Bell the rightful inventor?
    (a) Antonio Meucci (b) Johann Philipp Reis
    (c) Elisha Gray (d) Thomas Edison

11. Who was the first to broadcast and receive radio waves?
    (a) Joseph Henry
    (b) Gian Domenico Romagnosi
    (c) Nikola Tesla
    (d) Heinrich Rudolf Hertz

12. Who, on 14 May 1896, made communication by wireless telegraphy for the first time?
    (a) Guglielmo Marconi (b) William Preece
    (c) Jagdish Chandra Bose (d) Édouard Branly

13. When did *Doordarshan* first telecast in New Delhi?
    (a) 15 August 1959
    (b) 15 September 1959
    (c) 15 October 1959
    (d) 15 November 1959

14. On 19 December 1958, the first radio broadcast from space came from which first experimental satellite?
    (a) Project SCORE (b) SAREX
    (c) STS-9 (d) Skylab 3

15. What does the word *Fax* – a technology used to transfer copies of documents, using devices operating over the telephone network – stand for?
    (a) Face card (b) Far Action Xerox
    (c) Facet (d) Facsimile

16. Which was the world's first commercial geosynchronous communication satellite which provided the first scheduled transoceanic TV service?
    (a) EchoStar-1 (b) Horizons-1
    (c) Intelset 1 (d) Syncom 1

17. Who shared the Nobel Prize with Marconi in 1909 for developing the wireless telegraphy?
    (a) Mahlon Loomis (b) Lee Deforest
    (c) Nikola Tesla (d) Karl Ferninand Braun

18. Which programming language is named after a British mathematician and astronomer who was the first legitimate child of the poet Lord Byron and his wife, Anne Isabella Milbanke?
    (a) Adenine (b) Alice
    (c) Ada (d) Agora

19. Who invented the FORTRAN (FORmula TRANslation) programming language in the mid 1950s?
    (a) John Kemeny (b) John Backus
    (c) Dennis Ritchie (d) Grace Hopper

20. Which American electronics engineer was the inventor of *Cray 1* computer who made the use of transistors in computers and later developed massive supercomputers?
    (a) James Gosling (b) Brendan Eich
    (c) Anders Hejlsberg (d) Seymour Cray

21. Completed on 21 January 1946, which was the first modern computer designed by John Mauchly and John Eckert?
    (a) ILLIAC (b) TIFRAC
    (c) ENIAC (d) ERMIAC

22. Who on 10 November 1983 created the first computer virus?
    (a) Fred Cohen (b) Bob Thomas
    (c) David L. Smith (d) John von Neumann

23. Who introduced the web browser on 26 February 1991 with the help of 'http'?
    (a) Brendan Eich
    (b) Douglas Adams
    (c) Marc Andreessen
    (d) Sir Timothy John Berners

24. Which two computer scientists formed the Apple Computer Company on 1 April 1976?
    (a) John Vincent Atanasoff and Jean Bartik
    (b) Dorothy E. Denning and Jack Dongarra
    (c) Adele Goldberg and Ian Goldberg
    (d) Steve Wozniak and Steve Jobs

25. Who wrote the first PC virus code on 30 January 1982?
    (a) John von Neumann (b) Fred Cohen
    (c) Richard Skrenta (d) Michael Crichton

26. *Robot* is a Czech word meaning *work*, but which famous science fiction writer first used the word *robotics* in 1941 to describe the technology of robots and predicted the rise of a powerful robot industry?
    (a) Harry Clement Stubbs (b) Arthur C. Clarke
    (c) Issac Asimov (d) Ray Cummings

27. Who invented the computer mouse, named because of its tail-like cable?
    (a) Tom Cranston (b) Doug Engelbart
    (c) Fred Longstaff (d) Kenyon Taylor

28. On 2 July 1900, who had flown the first airship LZ-1, world's first untethered rigid airship carrying five passengers?
    (a) Francesco Lana de Terzi
    (b) Jean-Pierre Blanchard
    (c) Henri Giffard
    (d) Count Ferninand von Zeppelin

29. On 21 May 1927, which famous aviator made the first solo non-stop flight between New York and Paris?
    (a) Dr. Hugo Eckener (b) John LaMountain
    (c) Charles Lindbergh (d) Thaddeus S. C. Lowe

30. Who on 7 December 1903 flew for twelve seconds for a distance of 120 feet at Kitty Hawk, North Carolina, USA in the first successful sustained powered flight in a heavier-than-air machine?
    (a) Alphonse Penaud
    (b) Gustave Whitehead
    (c) Lawrence Hargrave
    (d) Wilbur and Orville Wright

DISCOVERIES AND INVENTIONS

1. Which French physicist and mathematician gave a combined theory of electricity and magnetism?
   (a) Alessandro Volta (b) Hans Christian Oersted
   (c) Michael Faraday (d) André-Marie Ampère

2. Who discovered the connection of electricity and magnetism by experiments involving a compass and electric circuits in 1820?
   (a) Hans Christian Andersen (b) Hans Christian Orsted
   (c) Johann Wilhelm Ritter (d) André-Marie Ampère

3. Who discovered the two types of static electricity, and that like charges repel each other whilst unlike charges attract?
   (a) William Gilbert (b) Sir Charles Parsons
   (c) Joseph Swan (d) Charles Du Fay

4. Who discovered the law, named after him, that at the same temperature and pressure equal volumes of all perfect gases contain the same number of particles?
   (a) Benoît Paul Émile Clapeyron
   (b) August Karl Krönig
   (c) Count Amedeo Avogadro
   (d) Nicolas Léonard Sadi Carnot

5. Which Serbian-born American physicist, regarded as America's greatest electrical engineer, designed and built the first alternating current induction motor in 1883, besides inventing an induction coil named after him?
   (a) Michael Faraday (b) François Arago
   (c) Galileo Ferraris (d) Nicola Tesla

6. Which Hungarian-born American physicist discovered the principle of the nuclear chain reaction and with Enrico Fermi created the first self-sustaining nuclear reactor in 1942?
   (a) Ernest Walton (b) Lise Meitner
   (c) Leo Szilard (d) Lew Kowarski

7. Which Russian physiologist and psychologist won the 1904 Nobel Prize in Medicine for his work on the physiology of digestion?
   (a) Franz Joseph Gall (b) Eduard Pernkopf
   (c) Josef Skoda (d) Ivan Petrovich Pavlov

8. Who discovered the Human Immunodeficiency Virus (HIV), a virus responsible for Acquired Immunodeficiency Syndrome (AIDS) independent of the French scientist Luc Montagnier?
   (a) Robert C. Gallo (b)William N. Rom
   (c) Harald zur Hausen (d) Françoise Barré-Sinoussi

9. Which German physicist discovered the dark lines in the solar spectrum and found the chemical composition of the Sun's atmosphere?
   (a) Charles Wheatstone (b) Gustav Kirchhoff
   (c) Anders Jonas Ångström (d) Joseph von Fraunhofer

10. Which British archaeologist and Egyptologist discovered the tomb of King Tutankhamen on 27 November 1922?
   (a) Howard Carter (b) Somaia Ismail
   (c) Sahar Saleem (d) Carsten Pusch

11. Who invented the automatic safety brake for elevators in 1854?
    (a) Richard Spikes (b) Josiah Maize
    (c) Elisha Graves Otis (d) Jesse Reno

12. Who designed the world's first hovercraft SR-N1 at Cowes, England in 1956?
    (a) Christopher Cockerell (b) Emanuel Swedenborg
    (c) Dagobert Müller (d) Toivo J. Kaario

13. Who designed the first electron microscope in 1931, but had to wait for fifty-five years to get the Nobel Prize, the longest for a scientist?
    (a) Ernst Ruska (b) Max Knoll
    (c) James Hillier (d) Zaccharias Janssen

14. The first prototype of which means of transport, supported on a cushion of air supplied by a powered fan mounted on the craft, was invented by Christopher Cockerell in 1956?
    (a) Amphebian car (b) Water trailer
    (c) Automobile ferry (d) Hovercraft

15. Who was the inventor of the Polaroid camera, the first 'instant camera', which he demonstrated on 21 February 1947 in New York City?
    (a) Samuel Shlafrock (b) Johann Heinrich Schultz
    (c) Sergei Lvovich Levitsky (d) Edwin Herbert Land

16. Who was the inventor of food canning, and discovered the process that kept foods from spoiling?
    (a) Peter Durand (b) Nicolas Appert
    (c) John Hall (d) Bryan Donkin

17. Who, on 22 October 1938, perfected the first Xerox copy?
    (a) Paul Selenyi (b) Gary Starkweather
    (c) Otto Kornei (d) Chester Carlson

18. Which type of camera lens was invented by F.G. Back, who was issued the first US patent for this optical device on 23 November 1948?
    (a) Photochromic lens (b) Wide angle lens
    (c) Zoom lens (d) Anti-fogging lens

19. Which German mechanical engineer invented the spark plug, the clutch, the gear shift, and the carburetor?
    (a) Gottlieb Daimler (b) Wilhelm Maybach
    (c) Karl Friedrich Benz (d) Emil Jellinek-Mercedes

20. Which device was invented in 1923 by Walther Banersfeld to project images of celestial objects onto the dome inside a theater for the viewers?
    (a) Planetary Equatorium (b) OmniMax movie system
    (c) Projection Planetarium (d) Digital Planetarium

21. Who invented the hot-air balloon and conducted the first public demonstration of the same on 4 June 1783, covering two kilometres in ten minutes?
    (a) Abert Read (b) Jim Mollison
    (c) João Ribeiro de Barros (d) Montgolfier brothers

22. Which Russian-born American aviation pioneer designed the first four-engine fixed-wing aircraft and the first successful helicopter of the most common configuration?
    (a) Andrei Tupolev (b) Paul E. Williams
    (c) Pavel Sukhoi (d) Igor Ivanovich Sikorsky

23. Which Russian airplane builder designed more than fifty airplanes including Il-2 Stormovik, jet airliner Il-62, and Aeroflot?
    (a) Sergei Ilyushin (b) Pavel Sukhoi
    (c) Andrei Tupolev (d) Artiom Mikoyan

24. Which German physicist discovered the dark lines in the solar spectrum and found the chemical composition of the Sun's atmosphere?
    (a) Charles Wheatstone (b) Gustav Kirchhoff
    (c) Joseph von Fraunhofer (d) Anders Jonas Ångström

25. Microphone was invented by Alexander Graham Bell in 1876, but who coined the term *microphone*?
    (a) David Hughes (b) Zacharis Janssen
    (c) Thomas Alva Edison (d) Charles Cross

26. Joseph Nicéphore Niepce of France is associated with which invention in photography?
    (a) Photography on film (b) Photography on silk
    (c) Photography on paper (d) Photography on metal

27. In which year was Dolly the sheep cloned at Roslin Institute?
    (a) 1991 (b) 1994
    (c) 1997 (d) 2001

28. Which physicist, among the following, was not involved in the discovery of quantum electrodynamics?
    (a) Richard Feynman (b) Niels Bohr
    (c) Julian Schwinger (d) Sin-Itiro Tomonaga

29. In 2010, paleontologists discovered a finger bone fragment of a female who is believed to have lived about 41,000 years ago and is an extinct species of human that lived alongside Neanderthals and the ancestors of people living today. By what name is this Paleolithic-era members of the genus *Homo* called?
    (a) *Homo habilis* (b) *Denisovans*
    (c) *Homo erectus* (d) *Orrorin tugenensis*

30. The biggest scientific news of the year 2012 was the discovery of Higgs Boson on 4 July at the European Organization for Nuclear Research (CERN). Which, among the following, is not true about this 'God Particle'?
    (a) Its symbol is H^o
    (b) It has zero spin, zero electric charge, and zero colour charge
    (c) It gives matter mass via an associated 'Higgs field'
    (d) None of these

ASTRONOMY AND UNIVERSE

1. Who was the discoverer of the ninth planet 'Pluto', now a dwarf planet, in 1930?
   (a) William H. Pickering (b) Percival Lowell
   (c) William Tombaugh (d) Urbain Le Verrier

2. Which dwarf planet, larger than Pluto, was discovered on 5 January 2005 by Michael E. Brown, Chad Trujillo, and David L. Rabinowitz at the Palomar Observatory?
   (a) Eris (b) Juno
   (c) Davida (d) Europa

3. Which is the biggest satellite in our solar system, discovered by Galileo on 7 January 1610?
   (a) Naptune's Triton (b) Uranus' Titania
   (c) Jupiter's Ganymede (d) Saturn's Titan

4. Having a diameter of 925 km, which is the largest asteroid in our Solar system?
   (a) Pallas (b) Vesta
   (c) Ceres (d) Hygiea

5. Deimos and Phobos are the satellites of which planet?
   (a) Jupiter (b) Neptune
   (c) Uranus (d) Mars

6. If all the planets fall into a hypothetical ocean, which one will float in water?
   (a) Mercury (b) Saturn
   (c) Venus (d) Uranus

7. Who discovered four satellites of the planet Saturn: Iapetus (1671), Rhea (1672), Tethys (1684) and Dione (1684)?
   (a) Jacques Cassini (b) Godefroy Wendelin
   (c) Galileo Galilei (d) Giovanni Domenico Cassini

8. Which 16th century German astronomer catalogued a large number of stars and proved that the moon's orbit was not circular, but elliptic?
   (a) Erasmus Reinhold (b) Johann Gottfried Galle
   (c) Johann Franz Encke (d) Karl Ludwig Hencke

9. Which contemporary of Newton built the first reflecting telescope, suggested rotation of Jupiter on its axis, and proposed the wave theory of light to explain diffraction?
   (a) Simon Marius (b) Robert Hooke
   (c) Heinrich Olbers (d) Urbain Le Verrier

10. Name the French astronomer who established alphanumeric names for the objects M1, M2, etc., notations?
    (a) Asaph Hall (b) Jeremiah Horrocks
    (c) Charles Messier (d) Frank Drake

11. Which German-born British astronomer, the most famous astronomer of the 18th century, discovered the planet Uranus and its two moons: Oberon, and Titania, as also two moons of Saturn: Mimas and Enceladus?
    (a) Martin Herschel (b) Caroline Herschel
    (c) John Herschel (d) Sir William Herschell

12. Who discovered the first asteroid 'Ceres'?
    (a) François Arago (b) Karl Ludwig Hencke
    (c) Giuseppe Piazzi (d) Lubos Kohoutek

13. Who discovered pulsars (pulsating stars) in 1966?
    (a) Thomas Gold (b) Jocelyn Bell
    (c) Karl Schwarzschild (d) Edwin Powell Hubble

14. Parsec – the distance at which a star would show a parallax of one second of arc – is equal to:
    (a) 3.26 light-years
    (b) 19,150,000,000,000 miles
    (c) 206,265 astronomical units
    (d) All the above

15. What are the brilliant points seen along the edge of the Moon's dark disk at a total solar eclipse, just before and just after actual totality?
    (a) Halo (b) Gould's Belt
    (c) Halation Ring (d) Baily's Beads

16. Which is the largest reflecting telescope in the world at present?
    (a) 387-in Keck telescope at Mauna Kea Observatory in Hawaii
    (b) Palomar 18-inch (460 mm) Schmidt optical reflecting telescope
    (c) Mount Wilson 100-inch (2.5 m) optical reflecting telescope
    (d) Hubble 2.4m space Telescope

17. Which is the only planet where poles are hotter than its equator?
    (a) Saturn (b) Uranus
    (c) Mercury (d) Neptune

18. The existence of the Andromeda Galaxy was announced in 1924 by Edwin Hubble. This neighbour of Milky Way is also known as:
    (a) M31 (b) NGC 224
    (c) Messier 31 (d) All the above

19. Which comet was first observed by a Czech astronomer on 7 March 1975, named after him, considered the most spectacular comet of the 21st century?
    (a) Kohoutek (b) Hyakutake
    (c) Elenin (d) Machholz

20. Which comet smashed into the surface of Jupiter on 17 July 1994, which created a giant dark spot over 12,000 km across, and released an energy equivalent to 6,000,000 megatons of TNT, that was about 800 times the world's nuclear arsenal?
    (a) Borrelly (b) Elenin
    (c) Hartley (d) Shoemaker-Levy 9

21. Which is the highest point on Mars at an elevation of 21,229 metres, as also the highest mountain in the solar system and the solar system's largest volcano?
    (a) Boosaule Montes
    (b) Maxwell Montes
    (c) Tharsis Bulge
    (d) Olympus Mons

22. Which rapidly spinning neutron star, about 20 km in diameter and having a mass of about 1.4 times that of the Sun, is the source of radio waves emitted as intense pulses at very precise intervals?
    (a) Quaser (b) Pulser
    (c) White dwarf (d) Red dwarf

23. Which Belgian astronomer and cosmologist was the originator of 'Big Bang' theory of Universe published in 1927?
    (a) Willem de Sitter (b) Edwin Hubble
    (c) Tullio Levi-Civita (d) George Lemaetre

24. Which British cosmologist, working with Hermann Bondi and Thomas Gold, proposed the steady state theory in the 1940s?
    (a) Jayant Narlikar (b) Fred Hoyle
    (c) Jocelyn Bell (d) William Alfred Fowler

25. Which project under the leadership of Francis Drake began in April 1960 for searching the signals of possible extraterrestrial intelligence?
    (a) Project SETI (b) Project Ozma
    (c) Project Cyclops (d) SERENDIP

26. Who was the first to put forward an idea of a body so massive that even light could not escape from it, now known as 'black hole'?
    (a) Karl Schwarzschild (b) Pierre-Simon Laplace
    (c) David Finkelstein (d) John Michell

27. What rare phenomenon occurs only thirteen to fourteen times in a century, when Mercury comes between the Sun and the Earth, making the former look like a small black dot moving across the face of the Sun?
    (a) Aphelion of Mercury (b) Perihelion of Mercury
    (c) Occultation of Mercury (d) Transit of Mercury

28. What occupies a compact region above the equator and is populated by protons of energies in the 10-100 Mev range? It can be a hazard to astronauts.
    (a) Kuiper Belt (b) Van Allen Belt
    (c) Stratosphere (d) Troposphere

29. Which near-earth asteroid with an estimated diameter of about 45 metres appeared in Earth's atmosphere on 15 February 2013, nearer than many artificial satellites?
    (a) 99942 Apophis (b) (29075) 1950 DA
    (c) 2011 MD (d) 2012 DA14

30. Which radio telescope that has taken the temperature of the universe in January 2013 found that it has cooled down, as per the prediction of the Big Bang theory?
    (a) Arecibo radio telescope
    (b) Hubble telescope
    (c) Australia telescope compact
    (d) Millimetre-wave telescopes

SPACE EXPLORATION

ɞ

1. Launched on 4 October 1957, which was the first artificial Earth satellite which orbited the Earth?
   (a) Sputnik 1 (b) Vanguard 1
   (c) Explorer 1 (d) Astérix

2. On 3 November 1957, which dog, the first animal in Earth's orbit, was carried out by former USSR's second artificial satellite by Sputnik 2?
   (a) Smelaya (b) Snezhinka
   (c) Laika (d) Lisa

3. Which country launched four satellites in orbit on a single rocket for the first time on 10 January 2007?
   (a) Canada (b) Japan
   (c) China (d) India

4. Name the comet from which NASA's Stardust mission, launched on 7 February 1999, brought back cosmic dust from it to Earth on 15 January 2006?
   (a) Tempel 1 (b) Borrelly
   (c) Wild 2 (d) Encke

5. Launched on 28 May 1971, which was the first spacecraft to soft land on Mars on 2 December 1971?
   (a) Cosmos 419 (Mars 1971C)
   (b) NASA's Mars Pathfinder
   (c) Viking 2
   (d) Mars Polar Lander

6. Which was the first successful exploration to explore Jupiter?
   (a) Pioneer 10 (b) Pioneer 11
   (c) Voyager 1 (d) Voyager 2

7. Name the first space station, which was launched by the USA in 1973?
   (a) Expedition 29
   (b) Skylab
   (c) Almaz
   (d) International Space Station

8. Name the nuclear-powered space mission, launched by the Atlas V rocket on 27 November 2011 by the NASA from the Kennedy Space Centre to explore the Martian soil and rocks?
   (a) Opportunity (b) Curiosity
   (c) Spirit (d) Humanity

9. Which became the first artificial object to leave the solar system?
   (a) Pioneer 10 (b) Pioneer 11
   (c) Voyager 1 (d) Voyager 2

10. Who became the first US woman in space on Space Shuttle Challenger's STS-7 mission on 18 June 1983?
    (a) Judith Resnik (b) Kathryn D. Sullivan
    (c) Anna Lee Fisher (d) Sally Ride

11. Who was America's first astronaut and second human in the world on a fifteen-minute sub-orbital flight in space on 5 May 1961?
    (a) John Glenn (b) Mark Shuttleworth
    (c) Alan B. Shepard, Jr (d) Scott Carpenter

12. Who was the first woman in space in Vostok-6 in 1963 which orbited the Earth 48 times in 71 hours?
    (a) Tatyana Kuznetsova (b) Svetlana Savitskaya
    (c) Valentina Tereshkova (d) Marsha Ivins

13. Who is known to have fifty hours and forty minutes of spacewalk time to her credit in seven walks, recorded as recently as 5 September 2012, the maximum by a female asrronaut?
    (a) Sunita Williams (b) Susan J. Helms
    (c) Janice E. Voss (d) Tamara E. Jernigan

14. Who is the world's oldest astronaut who went on board Discovery US STS-95, launched on 29 October 1998, at the age of 77?
    (a) John Glenn (b) Mike Melvill
    (c) Dennis Tito (d) Franklin Chang-Diaz

15. Who was the first person to drive a vehicle on the Moon during the Apollo 15 mission?
    (a) James Irwin (b) Dave Scott
    (c) Alfred Worden (d) Richard F. Gordon, Jr.

16. In a spaceflight between 10 December 2006 and 22 June 2007, who holds the record for the longest single spaceflight by a woman (195 days)?
    (a) Peggy Whitson (b) Rhea Seddon
    (c) Sunita Williams (d) Tamara E. Jernigan

17. For how many days did Russian astronaut Valeri Polyakov remain in space to create a new record for the longest human spaceflight?
    (a) 326.5 days (b) 364.9 days
    (c) 379.6 days (d) 437.7 days

18. When Eugene Cernan and Harrison Schmitt landed on the moon for the last time on 11 December 1972 in Apollo 17 mission, who stayed in the lunar orbit for over six days, the maximum by any moon-orbiting astronaut?
    (a) Walter Schirra (b) David Scott
    (c) Ronald Evans (d) Thomas Stafford

19. Which Apollo space mission with the crew Jim Lovell, Fred Haise, John Swigert was aborted mid-way for lunar landing after an oxygen tank exploded? The lucky crew landed safely on earth after six days of its launch.
    (a) Apollo 13 (b) Apollo 14
    (c) Apollo 15 (d) Apollo 16

20. Who was the youngest astronaut or cosmonaut (25 years, 10 months, 24 days old) to go to space on 6 August 1961?
    (a) Thomas Stafford (b) Gherman Titov
    (c) Sally Ride (d) Vladimir Titov

21. Who was the first astronaut or cosmonaut to die while landing on 24 April 1967?
    (a) Vladislav Volkov (b) Georgi Dobrovolski
    (c) Viktor Patsayev (d) Vladimir Komarov

22. In which Apollo Programme did three astronauts Frank Borman, Jim Lovell, and Bill Anders circle the lunar orbit on 24 December 1968?
    (a) Apollo 7 (b) Apollo 8
    (c) Apollo 9 (d) Apollo 10

23. Who was the first female to spacewalk on 25 July 1984?
    (a) Svetlana Savitskaya (b) Kathryn D. Sullivan
    (c) Shannon Lucid (d) Linda M. Godwin

24. Having the same volume, which heavenly body among the following, is the heaviest in this universe?
    (a) White Dwarf (b) Our Sun
    (c) Neutron Star (d) Red Giant

25. As on 4 December 2012, who had spent the maximum total time in space (803 days) in his six flights?
    (a) Sergei Avdeyev (b) Alexandr Kaleri
    (c) Sergei Krikalev (d) Yuri Malenchenko

26. Which spacecraft gave the first pictures of the lunar far-side on 7 October 1959?
    (a) Luna 1 (b) Luna 2
    (c) Luna 3 (d) Luna 4

27. Which spacecraft had the first soft landing on Titan, the largest moon of Saturn on 14 January 2005?
    (a) Stardust (b) Huygens probe
    (c) Deep Impact (d) Hayabusa

28. Name the Chinese space mission in which the country's first astronaut Yang Liwei made an orbit on 15 October 2003?
    (a) Shenzhou (b) Dong Fang Hong I
    (c) Kuafu (d) Tiangong 2

29. Who was the first Briton to go in space?
    (a) Mae Jemison (b) Ellen Ochoa
    (c) Helen Sharman (d) Roberta Bondar

30. Which among the following options is <u>not correct</u> about the space flight on which Rakesh Sharma went to space in April 1984?
    (a) He became the first Indian to go to space
    (b) Four spacecrafts were employed for this purpose
    (c) Kathryn D. Sullivan was the only female astronaut
    (d) The first time the crew consisted of eleven people

NATIONAL AWARDS AND HONOURS

1. At 54, who was the youngest person alive at the time of receiving the Baharat Ratna award?
   (a) Indira Gandhi (b) Rajiv Gandhi
   (c) Aruna Asif Ali (d) Satyajit Ray

2. Who was the first person of foreign origin to win the Bharat Ratna?
   (a) Mother Teresa (b) Khan Abdul Gaffar Khan
   (c) Dr. Nelson Mandela (d) Dalai Lama

3. Who was the first person to be awarded the Bharat Ratna posthumously?
   (a) Kumarswami Kamraj (b) Acharya Vinoba Bhave
   (c) M.G. Ramachandram (d) Lal Bahadur Shastri

4. What is the correct order of precedence in Medals and Decorations during the course of presentation by the President of India?
   (a) Bharat Ratna-Padma Vibhushan-Padma Bhushan-Param Vir Chakra
   (b) Bharat Ratna-Param Vir Chakra-Ashok Chakra-Padma Vibhushan
   (c) Bharat Ratna-Padma Vibhushan-Param Vir Chakra-Ashok Chakra
   (d) Bharat Ratna-Param Vir Chakra-Param Vishisht Sewa Medal-Maha Vir Chakra

5. Who was awarded the first Param Vir Chakra, India's highest military decoration awarded for the highest degree of valour?
   (a) Lance Naik Karam Singh
   (b) Major Somnath Sharma
   (c) Major Dhan Singh Thapa
   (d) Group Captain Gurbachan Singh Salaria

6. Which wing of Indian defence was awarded the most Mahavir Chakras (11) in a single conflict during the Indo-Pakistan War of 1971?
   (a) Indian Army (b) Indian Air Force
   (c) Indian Navy (d) Indo-Tibetan Border Force

7. Which is the highest peacetime gallantry award, equivalent to Param Vir Chakra, for valour, courageous action or self-sacrifice away from the battlefield? It is the peace time equivalent of the Param Vir Chakra.
   (a) Shaurya Chakra (b) Kirti Chakra
   (c) Ashok Chakra (d) Vijay Chakra

8. In which field is the Tansen Award given for outstanding performance?
   (a) Indian classical music
   (b) Classical vocal music
   (c) Classical instrumental music
   (d) Classical Hindustani music

9. Which is the most prestigious literary award in India?
   (a) Kamal Kumari National Award
   (b) Saraswati Samman
   (c) Maharishi Badrayan Vyas Samman
   (d) Bhartiya Jnanpith Award

10. For which Indian language is Vachaspati Puruskar given?
    (a) Sanskrit (b) Hindi
    (c) Gujarati (d) Bengali

11. Who was the first recipient of Saraswati Samman?
    (a) Harivansh Rai 'Bachchan'
    (b) Ashapurna Devi
    (c) Firaq Gorakhpuri
    (d) Mahadevi Varma

12. Who was the first recipient of Sahitya Akademi Award in Hindi literature in 1955 when the award was instituted?
    (a) Rahul Sankrityayan
    (b) Acharya Narendra Dev
    (c) Sumitranandan Pant
    (d) Makhanlal Chaturvedi

13. Who was the first recipient of Dada Saheb Phalke Award?
    (a) Devika Rani Roerich
    (b) Kanan Devi
    (c) Durga Khote
    (d) Prithvi Raj Kapoor

14. Which state government instituted the Golden Nandi Film Awards?
    (a) Maharashtra (b) Gujarat
    (c) Andhra Pradesh (d) Tamil Nadu

15. The prestigious Filmfare Awards were first introduced in 1954. Which film won the best film award that year?
    (a) *Do Bigha Zameen*
    (b) *Mother India*
    (c) *Baiju Bawra*
    (d) *Naya Daur*

16. Which award for peace and international understanding was instituted by the Government of India for outstanding contribution to the promotion of international understanding and friendship among the peoples of the world?
    (a) Gandhi Peace prize
    (b) Jawaharlal Nehru Award for International Understanding
    (c) Indira Gandhi Prize for Peace, Disarmament and Development
    (d) Rajiv Gandhi Sadbhavana Award

17. The Kalinga prize was instituted for the popularisation of science and presented each year by UNESCO to a person with a distinguished career of service in the interpretation of science and research to the public. Who instituted this prize in 1952?
    (a) Jawahar Lal Nehru (b) Homi Jahagir Bhabha
    (c) Biju Patnaik (d) Nandini Satpathy

18. U Thant, former secretary general of UNO was the first recipient of the Jawharlal Nehru Award for International Understanding in 1965. Who was the first Indian to receive this award in 1969?
    (a) Aruna Asaf Ali (b) Vinoba Bhave
    (c) Mother Teresa (d) Indira Gandhi

19. Which among the following is not a bravery award given to children between 6 and 18 years of age?
    (a) Sanjay Chopra Award
    (b) Geeta Chopra Award
    (c) Bapu Gayadhani Award
    (d) Nirbhaya Award

20. Which among the following option is <u>not correct</u> about the Shanti Swarup Bhatnagar Prize for Science and Technology?
    (a) The award is given by the Indian Science Academy
    (b) The age limit of the scientist should not be more than 45
    (c) This is the highest award in science and technology in India
    (d) The award winner gets Rs 500,000 besides citation

21. To mark the completion of fifty years of Independence, which Indian was honoured by Pakistan with *Nishan-e-Imtiaz*, her highest civilian award ?
    (a) Ismat Chughtai (b) Amrita Pritam
    (c) Dilip Kumar (d) Firaq Gorakhpuri

22. Who was the first woman to be honoured with the Jnanpith Award in 1976, the most prestigious literary honour in the country?
    (a) Ashapoorna Devi (b) Qurratulain Hyder
    (c) Amrita Pritam (d) Mahadevi Varma

23. Who was the second Indian to become Miss Universe?
    (a) Sushmita Sen (b) Lara Datta
    (c) Aishwarya Rai (d) Priyanka Chopra

24. Which pair hosted the 11th Indian Television Awards in 2012?
    (a) Vishal Malhotra and Mona Singh
    (b) Ram Kapoor and Roshni Chopra
    (c) Ronit Roy and Ram Kapoor
    (d) Ronit Roy and Meghna Malik

25. In which field is the Rafi Ahmed Kidwai Award, instituted in 1956, given?
    (a) Agriculture (b) Industry
    (c) Education (d) Computer Science

26. Which among the following awards is India's highest honour given for achievement in sports?
    (a) Arjun Award
    (b) Dronacharya Award
    (c) Dhyan Chand Award
    (d) Rajiv Gandhi Khel Ratna Award

27. Who among the following was not the first recipient of the Dhyan Chand Award (2002), India's highest award for lifetime achievement in sports and games, given by the Government of India?
    (a) Ashok Diwan (b) Aparna Ghosh
    (c) Shahuraj Birajdar (d) Charles Cornelius

28. In which year were the Arjuna Awards instituted for sportspersons?
    (a) 1959 (b) 1960
    (c) 1961 (d) 1962

29. Who was the first politician to be honourd by the NDTV Awards in 2005?
    (a) Sonia Gandhi (b) Narendra Modi
    (c) Sheila Dixit (d) Dr. Manmohan Singh

30. Which state government of India presents the Kalidas Samman, a prestigious arts award every year?
    (a) Uttar Pradesh (b) Madhya Pradesh
    (c) Tamil Nadu (d) Uttarakhand

INTERNATIONAL AWARDS AND HONOURS

1. Who was the first woman to be awarded the Nobel Prize for Physiology or Medicine?
   (a) Gerty Theresa Cori
   (b) Maria Goeppert-Mayer
   (c) Barbara McClintock
   (d)Dorothy Crowfoot Hodgkin

2. Who was first ever American to win the Nobel Prize in 1906?
   (a) Harold Urey
   (b) Theodore Roosevelt
   (c) Pearl Buch
   (d) Albert Abraham Michelson

3. Who was the first woman winner of the Nobel Prize for Literature in 1945?
   (a) Gabriela Mistral
   (b) Nelly Sachs
   (c) Nadine Gardimer
   (d) Wislawa Szymborska

4. At 25, who was the youngest Nobel Laureate?
   (a) Werner Heisenberg (b) Max Plank
   (c) Sir Lawrence Bragg (d) Paul Dirac

5. Who is the only father-son duo to share a Nobel Prize?
   (a) Sir William Bragg and Sir Lawrence Bragg
   (b) Karl Siegbahn and Kai Manne Borje Siegbahn
   (c) Niels Bohr and his son Aage Bohr
   (d) Joseph John Thomson and George Paget Thomson

6. Which International Agency and its Director General, Mohamed ElBaradei, were jointly awarded the 2005 Nobel Peace Prize?
   (a) UN High Commissioner for Refugees
   (b) International Atomic Energy Agency
   (c) International Committee of the Red Cross
   (d) The Pugwash Conferences on Science and World Affairs

7. Who is the only person to win two Nobel Prizes in Chemistry and Peace?
   (a) John Bardeen (b) Frederick Sanger
   (c) Linus Pauling (d) Marie Curie

8. Which Dutch chemist was awarded the very first Nobel Prize for Chemistry in 1901 for his discovery of the laws of chemical dynamics and osmosis pressure in solutions?
   (a) Peter Debye
   (b) Paul Crutzen
   (c) Willem Einthoven
   (d) Jacobus nan't Hoff

9. Who was the first Japanese to be awarded the Nobel Prize in 1949?
   (a) Leo Esaki (b) Eisaku Sato
   (c) Hideki Yukawa (d) Hideki Shirakawa

10. In which year did Subramanyam Chandrasekhar, the Indian-born American astro-physicist shared the Nobel Prize with William Fowler for "the theoretical studies of the physical processes of importance to the structure and evolution of the stars"?
    (a) 1981 (b) 1982
    (c) 1983 (d) 1984

11. Who in 1998 received the Nobel Prize for his work on famine, human development theory, welfare economics, the underlying mechanisms of poverty, and political liberalism?
    (a) Milton Friedman (b) Myron Scholes
    (c) Jan Tinbergen (d) Prof. Amartya Sen

12. Who was the first winner of the Nobel Prize for Physics in 1901?
    (a) Hendrik A. Lorentz (b) Pieter Zeeman
    (c) John W. Strutt (d) Wilhelm Conrad Röntgen

13. Who shared the 1903 Nobel Prize for Physics with Marie Curie and Pierre Curie?
    (a) Adolf von Baeyer (b) Henri Becquerel
    (c) Gabriel Lippmann (d) Nils G. Dalen

14. Who became the first person to be awarded the Nobel Prize for the second time?
    (a) Maria Goeppert-Mayer (b) Rosalyn Yalow
    (c) Irene Joliot-Curie (d) Marie Curie

15. Who was the first Asian scientist to be awarded the Nobel Prize for Physics in 1930?
    (a) Hideki Yukawa (b) Makoto Kobayashi
    (c) Toshihide Maskawa (d) Sir C.V. Raman

16. For which discovery was Victor Franz Hess awarded the Nobel Prize for Physics in 1935?
    (a) Background radiation (b) Cosmic rays
    (c) Microwaves (d) Cerenkov radiations

17. For which discovery was Carl David Anderson awarded the Nobel Prize for Physics in 1935?
    (a) Positron (b) Leptons
    (c) Graviton (d) Bosons

18. Who won the Nobel Prize in 1967 for his contributions to the theory of nuclear reactions, especially his discoveries concerning the energy production in stars?
    (a) Theodore von Kármán
    (b) Klaus Fuchs
    (c) Hans Albrecht Bethe
    (d) Kurt Gottfried

19. Who was the second woman to receive the Nobel Prize in physics, following Marie Curie?
    (a) Barbara McClintock
    (b) Dorothy Crowfoot Hodgkin
    (c) Gertrude Elion
    (d) Maria Geoppert Mayer

20. He was just 31 when he won the Nobel Prize in 1932 for the creation of quantum mechanics, the application of which has led to the discovery of the allotropic forms of hydrogen. Who was this German physicist, most famous for his uncertainty principle?
    (a) Paul A.M. Dirac (b) Erwin Schrodinger
    (c) Werner Heisenberg (d) Arthur H. Compton

21. Who is the only Nobel Laureate to have won two Nobel Prizes in physics?
    (a) Frederic Sanger (b) Linus Pauling
    (c) John Bardeen (d) Marie Curie

22. Which country has won most titles (8) of Miss Universe since its inception in 1952?
    (a) U.S.A. (b) Venezuela
    (c) Puerto Rico (d) Sweden

23. Created by Eric Morley from the United Kingdom in 1951, which is the oldest surviving major international beauty pageant?
    (a) Miss World (b) Miss Europe
    (c) Miss Earth (d) Miss International

24. Who was the first Academy Award winner in history in 1929 as the Best Actor for his role in the movie *The Last Command*?
    (a) Emil Jannings (b) Gary Cooper
    (c) Richard Arlen (d) Charles "Buddy" Rogers

25. Who was the first winner from India to win the Ramon Magsaysay Award in 1958?
    (a) Satyajit Ray (b) C.D. Deshmukh
    (c) Vinoba Bhave (d) Verghese Kurien

26. Which award, established in 1929 by the American Society of Mechanical Engineers, is given for "distinguished achievement in management and service to the community"?
    (a) Enterprise Initiative Award
    (b) The Malcolm Baldrige National Quality Award
    (c) Shingo Prize
    (d) The Henry Laurence Gantt Medal

27. Which among the following films of Satyajit Ray was the first to win the Best Film from any Source (for non-British films) by the British Academy of Film and Television Arts (BAFTA)?
    (a) *The Unvanquished* (b) *The World of Apu*
    (c) *Song of the Road* (d) *Pather Panchali*

28. Mother Teresa was the first winner of which award in 1973, six years before she got the Nobel Peace Prize, "for her extraordinary efforts to help the homeless and neglected children of Calcutta, which inspired millions of others around the world"?
    (a) The Balzan Prize
    (b) Ramon Magsaysay Award
    (c) TheTempleton Prize
    (d) The Pope John XXIII Peace Prize
29. In which field of sports is *The Golden Foot award* given to players who stand out for their athletic achievements?
    (a) Basketball (b) Baseball
    (c) Boxing (d) Football

30. Who was the first Indian novelist to win the Man Booker Prize for Fiction?
    (a) Salman Rushdie (b) Arundhati Roy
    (c) Kiran Desai (d) Aravind Adiga

SPORTS IN INDIA

☙

1. Which among the following trophies is not given away in the game of cricket?
   (a) Deodhar Trophy (b) Ghulam Ahmed Trophy
   (c) Irani Trophy (d) Rothman's Trophy

2. Which among the following trophies is not associated with hockey?
   (a) Maharaj Prithi Singh Cup
   (b) Rangaswami Cup
   (c) Rene Frank Trophy
   (d) Obaidullah Gold Cup

3. Other than hockey, in which Olympic sport India participated as a team but could not advance to the second round at the 1948 London Olympics?
   (a) Football (b) Basketball
   (c) Polo (d) Water Polo

4. India regained the Olympic hockey title at the 1964 Tokyo Olympic Games by defeating Pakistan by a solitary gold, but not before struggling in the Group B matches where India managed 1-1 ties with Spain and United Germany. Who scored the winning goal for India to fetch her seventh Olympic gold medal?
   (a) Charanjit Singh (b) Prithipal Singh
   (c) Mohinder Lal (d) Leslie Claudius

5. In which shooting event did Major Rajyavardhan Rathore win a silver medal at the 2004 Summer Olympics in Athens, thus becoming the first ever Indian to win a medal in Olympic shooting?
   (a) Skeet
   (b) Trap
   (c) Double trap
   (d) Ten metre running target

6. Against which nation did Sachin Tendulkar hit his hundredth century in international cricket, the maximum by a cricketer?
   (a) England (b) Bangladesh
   (c) West Indies (d) Sri Lanka

7. Which Indian won the 2010 Commonwealth games in the women's individual recurve event as also won gold medal in the same competition in the women's team recurve event along with two other women archers?
   (a) Dola Banerjee (b) Bombayala Devi
   (c) Vidya Kumari (d) Deepika Prajapati

8. In which track and field event did Lavy Pinto of India achieve the distinction of multiple gold medals?
   (a) 100m and 200m sprint
   (b) 200m and 400m race
   (c) Long Jump and Triple Jump
   (d) Shot Put and Discus Throw

9. At which Asian Games did Milkha Singh win two gold medals, in 200m and 400m?
   (a) 1954, Manila (b) 1958, Tokyo
   (c) 1962, Jakarta (d) 1966, Bangkok

10. Who was the first Indian woman to win gold medal at any Asian Games?
    (a) P.T. Usha (b) Shiny Abraham
    (c) Kamaljeet Sandhu (d) Rosa Kutty

11. Name the Indian weightlifter to defend her Gold Medal in the Women's 69 kg category of weightlifting at the 2010 Delhi Commonwealth Games?
    (a) Kunjarani Devi (b) Renu Bala Chanu Yumnam
    (c) Soniya Chanu (d) Karnam Malleshwari

12. What title used to be given to Wrestling Champion of India prior to modern styles of wrestling?.
    (a) *Rustam-e-Punjab* (b) *Rustam-i-Zamana*
    (c) *Bharat-Kesri* (d) *Rustam-i-Hind*

13. Who was the first Indian to win a Gold Medal in wrestling at the 1958 British Empire & Commonwealth Games held in Cardiff, Wales?
    (a) Lila Ram (b) Bishwanath Singh
    (c) Hukum Singh (d) Randhawa Singh

14. A Dronacharya Awardee in 2009 and a Padma Shri, a Gold Medalist at the 1982 Asian Games and a Bronze medalist in 1974 Asian Games, which famous Indian wrestler is dubbed as *Mahabali* who was coached by the famous wrestling coach Guru Hanuman in Delhi?
    (a) Chandagi Ram (b) Bhim Singh
    (c) Maruti Mane (d) Satpal Singh

15. In golf, who was the first winner of Indian Open in 1991?
    (a) Ali Sher (b) Jeev Milkha Singh
    (c) Gaurav Ghei (d) Arjun Atwal

16. Who was the first Indian to reach the quarter-finals of any Grand Slam in Singles (at Wimbledon)?
    (a) Sumant Mishra
    (b) Ghouse Mohammed
    (c) Mohammad Saleem
    (d) Sardar Nihal Singh

17. Which was the only time in hockey that India won the World Cup defeating Pakistan by a margin of 2-1?
    (a) 1971 in Barcelona, Spain
    (b) 1975 in Kuala Lumpur, Malaysia
    (c) 1998 in Utrecht, Holland
    (d) 2006 in Mönchengladbach, Germany

18. Who was the first ever Indian captain in T20?
    (a) Sachin Tendulkar (b) Virender Sehwag
    (c) Dinesh Mongia (d) M.S. Dhoni

19. In how many balls did Yuvraj Singh make the fastest half-century in T20?
    (a) 12 balls (b) 14 balls
    (c) 16 balls (d) 18 balls

20. Known as Sagol Kangjei, Kanjai-bazee, or Pulu, where in modern Northeast India was established the first polo club in 1834?
    (a) Imphal, Manipur (b) Aizawl, Mizoram
    (c) Shillong, Meghalaya (d) Silchar, Assam

21. Where in India was the game of badminton 'invented' around 1870 by the British?
    (a) Jaipur (b) Kolkata
    (c) Surat (d) Poona (Pune)

22. He won the Indian national title consecutively for eight years, was the men's singles gold medallist at the Commonwealth Games in Edmonton, Canada. We are talking of which player who is the first ever Indian to win the All England Championship in 1980?
    (a) Dinesh Khanna
    (b) Prakash Padukone
    (c) Nandu Natekar
    (d) Suresh Goel

23. Awarded with the Rajiv Gandhi Khel Ratna, which Indian player emulated the feat of Prakash Padukone to win the All England Open Badminton Championships in 2001 by defeating Chen Hong of China?
    (a) Chetan Anand
    (b) Syed Modi
    (c) Pullela Gopichand
    (d) Dipankar Bhattacharjee

24. Who is the first Indian woman to reach the singles semi-finals at the Olympics and the first Indian to win the World Junior Badminton Championships, besides becoming the first Indian to win a Super Series tournament, by clinching the prestigious Indonesia Open?
    (a) Madhumita Bisht (b) Aparna Popat
    (c) Ami Ghia (d) Saina Nehwal

25. Which Indian boxer won the gold medal at the Bangkok Asian Games (1998) in the 54 kg Bantamweight category by defeating Wong Prages Sontaya of Thailand who was World No. 3 at that time?
    (a) Diwakar Prasad (b) Dingko Singh
    (c) D.S. Yadav (d) Anthresh Lalit Lakra

26. This handsome boxer created history by winning a bronze medal at the 2008 Beijing Olympics, thus becoming the first ever Indian boxer to earn an Olympic medal. Who is this awardee of the Rajiv Gandhi Khel Ratna award?
    (a) Dinesh Kumar (b) Jitender Kumar
    (c) Akhil Kumar (d) Vijender Singh

27. Who is the reigning national snooker champion, besides being seven-time world title holder?
    (a) Aditya Mehta (b) Yasin Merchant
    (c) Ashok Shandilya (d) Pankaj Advani

28. Who became the first Indian to win the Amateur World Championship twice, in 1958 and 1964?
    (a) Satish Mohan (b) Michael Ferreira
    (c) Wilson Jones (d) Subhash Agrawal

29. As of 2012, who is the current World Chess Champion?
    (a) Veselin Topalov (b) Alexander Khalifman
    (c) Viswanathan Anand (d) Rustam Kasimdzhanov

30. In golf, who was the first winner of Indian Open in 1991?
    (a) Ali Sher (b) Jeev Milkha Singh
    (c) Gaurav Ghei (d) Arjun Atwal

WORLD OF SPORTS

ଓ

1. Which sport is Merdeka Cup associated with?
   (a) Hockey (b) Football
   (c) Volleyball (d) Badminton

2. Which among the following trophies is not associated with golf?
   (a) Walker Cup (b) Canada Cup
   (c) Wightman Cup (d) Eisenhower Cup

3. How many times has Martina Navratilova won the Wimbledon Singles' title from 1978 to 1990, thus establishing a new record?
   (a) Six (b) Seven
   (c) Eight (d) Nine

4. Which sport is Swaythling Cup associated with?
   (a) Badminton (b) Table Tennis
   (c) Lawn Tennis (d) Polo

5. Who became the youngest-ever champion at the 1990 French Open at the age of 16?
   (a) Monica Seles (b) Justine Henin
   (c) Billie Jean King (d) Gabrielia Sabatini

6. Who was the founder of the modern Olympic Games?
   (a) Dr. William Brooks (b) Baron Pierre de Coubertin
   (c) Thomas Arnold (d) Juan Antonio Samaranch

7. When was cricket introduced in the Olympic Games?
   (a) Paris, 1900 (b) London, 2008
   (c) London, 1948 (d) Melbourne, 1956

8. Spyridon was the first ever person to win a Gold medal in Marathon in 1896. Which country did he represent?
   (a) Greece (b) France
   (c) Belgium (d) Austria

9. In which Olympic Games was the Olympic Flag launched?
   (a) 1920, Antwerp (b) 1924, Paris
   (c) 1928, Amsterdam (d) 1932, Los Angeles

10. At the Opening Ceremony, which country leads the parade of nations?
    (a) Afghanistan (b) Greece
    (c) Winner of the last Game (d) The host country

11. Who broke the record of Bob Beamon's Long Jump of 8.90 metres by jumping 8.95 metres in 1991?
    (a) Ralf Boston (b) Carl Lewis
    (c) Mike Powell (d) Igor Ter-Ovanesyan

12. At which Olympic Games did Emil Zatopek of the then Czechoslovakia win the Gold medals in 5000m, 10,000m, and Marathon race?
    (a) 1948, London (b) 1952, Helsinki
    (c) 1956, Melbourne (d) 1960, Rome

13. Which Latin American nation won a gold medal in soccer at the 1928 Amsterdam Olympics?
    - (a) Brazil
    - (b) Argentina
    - (c) Uruguay
    - (d) Paraguay

14. Name the first nation that won the first gold medal in women's hockey in 1980?
    - (a) Australia
    - (b) Great Britain
    - (c) Zimbabwe
    - (d) India

15. Which great athlete from Finland was the first person to win the 1500-5000m double in any edition of the Olympic Games?
    - (a) Paavo Nurmi
    - (b) Hannes Kolehmainen
    - (c) Ville Ritola
    - (d) Lauri Lehtinen

16. Who was the first Olympian to win nine gold medals in his Olympic appearances, then a record?
    - (a) Ian Thorpe
    - (b) Jesse Owens
    - (c) Paavo Nurmi
    - (d) Michael Phelps

17. Name the athlete who was the first and so far the only to win two Olympic golds in decathlon event twice in a row, in 1980 and 1984?
    - (a) Bob Mathias
    - (b) Daley Thompson
    - (c) Milt Campbell
    - (d) Bryan Clay

18. Which Russian-Ukrainian and former Soviet gymnast is the only female athlete to win nine Olympic gold medals?
    - (a) Polina Astakhova
    - (b) Larisa Semyonovna Latynina
    - (c) Ludmilla Tourischeva
    - (d) Nadia Comaneci

19. Philip Noel-Baker of Great Britain is the only Olympic medallist ever to be awarded the Nobel Peace Prize. In which athletic event did he win a silver medal?
    (a) 1500m (b) 5000m
    (c) 10,000m (d) Triple jump

20. Name the only tennis player who has won the Wimbledon ladies' singles title five times and won an Olympic silver medal in archery at the Olympics?
    (a) Dorothea Lambert Chambers
    (b) Steffi Graf
    (c) Helen Wills Moody
    (d) Charlotte "Lottie" Dod

21. Boxing was part of the ancient Olympic Games since 23rd Olympiad in 688 BC in which boxers used to wrap a leather strip around their hands. Which famous Greek mathematician was also among the winners in this type of boxing?
    (a) Anaxagoras (b) Pythagoras
    (c) Aristarchus (d) Euclid

22. Which Bulgaria-born Turkish weightlifter was the World Junior Champion in 1993 and Five-time World Champion from 1994 till 2003, and is one of the four weightlifters winning three consecutive gold medals at the Olympic Games (1996-2004)?
    (a) Ibrahim Elmali (b) Naim Suleymanoglu
    (c) Halil Mutlu (d) Adrian Jigau

23. Which country has won the World Cup Football five times (in 1958, 1962, 1970, 1994, 2002), the most number by any one, and is the only team to have played in every tournament?
    (a) Italy (b) Italy
    (c) Brazil (d) France

24. Voted 'Football Player of the Century' with 1281 goals to his credit, which great footballer won his first World Cup at the tender age of 17 and was the only footballer to be a part of three World Cup-winning squads?
    (a) Pele (b) Di Stefano
    (c) Puscas (d) Ronaldo

25. Who is regarded as the greatest heavyweight boxing champion of all time who had a fantastic record of his 71 fights during the period 1937–1949, the longest span of a heavyweight titleholder?
    (a) Ezzard Charles (b) Joe Louis
    (c) James J. Braddock (d) Floyd Patterson

26. With a tag of "most famous athlete in the world", Muhammad Ali was crowned "Sportsman of the Century" by *Sports Illustrated* in 1999. An Olympic gold medallist, Ali created history by regaining his crown after seven years on 30 October 1974. Name the champion whom Ali defeated?
    (a) Leon Spinks (b) Joe Bugner
    (c) Ken Norton (d) George Foreman

27. Who was the first official World Chess Champion, who claimed the title in 1886?
    (a) Wilhelm Steinitz (b) Jose Raul Capablanca
    (c) Max Euwe (d) Emanuel Lasker

28. Till 2012, which Chinese player was the reigning Women's World Chess Champion?
    (a) Xie Jun (b) Xu Yuhua
    (c) Hou Yifan (d) Zhu Chen

29. Nicknamed 'The Golden Bear', who won 18 career major championships on the PGA Tour over a span of 25 years and is regarded as one of the greatest professional golfers of all time?
    (a) Sam Snead (b) Ben Hogan
    (c) Jack Nicklaus (d) Tiger Woods

30. Vijay Singh was the top-ranked golfer in 2004-05 for 32 weeks as per the Official World Golf Rankings. Which country does he belong to?
    (a) India (b) Canada
    (c) Britain (d) Fiji

MISCELLANY

1. Where was Thomas Alva Edison – the American inventor and the greatest inventor of all times with 1093 patents – born?
   (a) Milan, Italy (b) Paris, France
   (c) Lisbon, Portugal (d) Tokyo, Japan

2. Which French astronomer and politician, the first Mayor of Paris, was guillotined on 12 November 1793 during the French Revolution?
   (a) Jean-Sylvain Bailly
   (b) Marie François Sadi Carnot
   (c) Marie Antoinette
   (d) Antoine Lavoisier

3. Which French chemist and physicist, the co-discoverer of boron, set an altitude record of 22,942 feet during an ascent in a balloon with the aim of measuring the possible modifications of the composition of air?
   (a) Alessandro Volta (b) Béatrice Romand
   (c) Joseph Gay-Lussac (d) Antoine Lavoisier

4. Which chemist, inventor of the negative-positive photographic process, was also a Member of Parliament of England between 1832 and 1835?
   (a) William Fox Talbot (b) Thomas Wedgwood
   (c) Frederick Scott Archer (d) John Herschel

5. An advocate for atomic theory and contributor in the fields of statistical mechanics and statistical thermodynamics, which Austrian physicist, suffering from a depression bout, committed suicide on 5 September 1906?
   (a) Josef Loschmidt
   (b) Andreas von Ettingshausen
   (c) Joseph Stefan
   (d) Ludwig Eduard Boltzmann

6. Which British physicist, killed in action at the Battle of Suvla Bay, Gallipoli at the age of 28, discovered in 1913 a law that bears his name? The law correlates wavelength and atomic number, thus demonstrating the importance of atomic theory.
   (a) James Chadwick
   (b) Robert Andrews Millikan
   (c) George Johnstone Stoney
   (d) Henry Gwyn Jeffreys Moseley

7. Name the artificial language, conceived by the Polish physician and linguist Lazar Lewis Zamenhof?
   (a) Poliespo (b) Esperanto
   (c) Slovio (d) Mondial

8. Who is the only person in the world to be an astronaut as well as an aquanaut, who during the 45-day experiment, spent 30 days working on the ocean floor?
   (a) Alan Bean (b) David Scott
   (c) Scott Carpenter (d) Eugene Cernan

9. Along with Frank Drake, which famous science fiction writer designed the plaques on 'Pioneer 10' and 'Pioneer 11' for the purpose of greeting and informing any extraterrestrial intelligence after they left the solar system?
   (a) Isaac Asimov (b) Jules Verne
   (c) Carl Sagan (d) Jason Blizzard

10. Eastman had fascination for the letter 'K'. David Houston, a photographic inventor suggested 'Nodak'(for the company which prodúces photographic materials and equipments) as a nickname of his home state, North Dakota. How did Eastman name it?
    (a) Kodak (b) Kono
    (c) Korda (d) Konodk

11. Written in 1830 by Sarah Josepha Hale, which was the famous poem which made the first recorded sound, demonstrated by Thomas Alva Edison on 6 December 1877?
    (a) Humpty Dumpty (b) Mary had a Little Lamb
    (c) Baa, Baa, Black Sheep (d) Twinkle Twinkle Little Star

12. On 19 April 1906, which famous French chemist and a Nobel Laureate died in an accident while crossing the Rue Dauphine in Paris when his head crushed under the carriage wheel?
    (a) Victor Grignard (b) Pierre Curie
    (c) Louis Le Chatelier (d) Louis Jacques Thénard

13. Considered as the father of computer science and artificial intelligence, which computer scientist committed suicide after eating an apple laced with cyanide on 7 June 1954, at the age of forty-two?
    (a) Alan Turing (b) Ian Goldberg
    (c) Gordon Cormack (d) Manny M. Lehman

14. Born on 10 December 1815 and died at the age of thirty-six at the same age as her father the poet Lord Byron, who was the first computer programmer?
    (a) Grace Hopper (b) Henrietta Swan Leavitt
    (c) Grete Hermann (d) Augusta Ada King Lovelace

15. Which great British physicist, who propounded the wave theory of light was well acquainted with Greek, Latin, French, Italian, Hebrew, Syrian, Samaritan, Arabic, Persian, Turkish and Amharic?
    (a) Thomas Young (b) Simeon Denis Poisson
    (c) Christiaan Huygens (d) Augustin-Jean Fresnel

16. Which famous British biologist and philosopher, who made important connections between evolution and genetics, was the first Director of UNESCO, and a founding member of the World Wildlife Fund?
    (a) Sir Julian Huxley (b) Jaime Torres Bodet
    (c) John W. Taylor (d) Luther Evans

17. Who came up with the following slogan for advertising the box camera: "You press the button, we do the rest"?
    (a) William Henry Talbot (b) Edwin Land
    (c) George Eastman (d) Richard Leach Maddox

18. Which popular mouthwash is named after Joseph Lister for his work in antisepsis?
    (a) Listafresh (b) Biolist
    (c) JoLi (d) Listerine

19. Who was the inventor of a system of shorthand in 1837?
    (a) Samuel Taylor (b) Thomas Shelton
    (c) John Robert Gregg (d) Isaac Pitman

20. Which famous French ocean explorer and co-inventor of aqual-lung or scuba, also produced a television series using underwater television?
    (a) Dr. Sylvia Earle
    (b) Captain Jacques-Yves Cousteau
    (c) Dr. Robert Ballard
    (d) Dr Peter Auster

21. Which Polish-born American physicist, winner of the Nobel Prize in 1944, was the first scientist to propose the joint European laboratory CERN?
    (a) Wolfgang Pauli (b) Isodor Isaac Rabi
    (c) Cecil F. Powell (d) Sir Edward V. Appleton

22. Norbert Wiener, an American mathematician, was awarded a Ph.D. by Harvard at the age of eighteen. In 1948, which new interdisciplinary study of the structure of regulatory systems did he introduce, the sub-title of which is "control and communication in the animal and machine"?
    (a) System Dynamics (b) Organizational theory
    (c) Perceptual control theory (d) Cybernetics

23. Near which river in the Siberian region was exploded an asteroid or comet 5 to 10 kilometres in diameter on 30 June 1908, in which an estimated 80 million trees were destroyed over 2,150 square kilometres, but luckily no one was killed?
    (a) Chusovaya River (b) Tavda River
    (c) Tunguska River (d) Angara River

24. Which American nuclear physicist was instrumental in developing the hydrogen bomb in association with Stanislav Ulam in 1952?
    (a) John von Neumann (b) Edward Teller
    (c) Enrico Fermi (d) Albert Einstein

25. Where on 19 September 1957 was the first underground nuclear explosion conducted by the USA?
    (a) Las Vegas, Nevada (b) Rongerikatolls
    (c) Marshall Islands (d) Christmas Island

26. Launched on 9 November 2003, BrahMos – India's supersonic cruise missile that can be launched from submarines, ships, aircraft or land – is a joint collaboration between India and which other country?
    (a) Russia (b) Uzbekistan
    (c) Ukraine (d) Georgia

27. Which Russian physicist is considered the father of the Russian hydrogen bomb?
    (a) Georgy Flyorov
    (b) Igor Vasilyevich Kurchatov
    (c) Alexander Rushkin
    (d) Andrei Sakharov

28. Who dropped the first atomic bomb named "Little Boy" by B-29 bomber at its target Aioi Bridge, Hiroshima in Japan at 8:15:17 a.m. on 6 August 1945?
    (a) Thomas Wilson Ferebee (b) Charles W. Sweeney
    (c) Paul Tibbets (d) George Marquardt

29. Which indigenously-built main battle tank was inducted into the Indian Army on 7 August 2004?
    (a) Bhim (b) Arjun
    (c) Nakul (d) Yudhha

30. Where in New Mexico, USA was the first ever atomic bomb tested on 16 July 1945?
    (a) Albuquerque (b) Alamogordo
    (c) Santa Fe (d) Tucumcari

ANSWERS

INDIAN HISTORY

1b	2d	3c	4b	5d	6b	7b	8a
9b	10c	11d	12b	13d	14c	15c	16b
17d	18a	19b	20a	21d	22c	23d	24c
25b	26c	27a	28c	29a	30c	31a	32b
33a	34b	35b	36b	37d	38c	39b	40a

HISTORY OF THE WORLD

1c	2d	3c	4b	5a	6b	7c	8a
9b	10a	11c	12b	13c	14c	15a	16d
17a	18b	19a	20c	21c	22b	23d	24d
25a	26c	27c	28a	29c	30c	31c	32a
33b	34d	35d	36d	37c	38b	39c	40b

INDIAN GEOGRAPHY

1b	2c	3a	4c	5d	6c	7c	8c
9d	10c	11b	12a	13b	14d	15c	16d
17c	18b	19c	20c	21d	22b	23a	24c
25d	26d	27c	28a	29c	30d		

GEOGRAPHY OF THE WORLD

1d	2d	3c	4b	5d	6c	7a	8d
9a	10b	11b	12a	13a	14c	15a	16d
17a	18b	19b	20c	21b	22a	23d	24b
25a	26d	27b	28c	29d	30a		

INDIAN CONSTITUTION

1c	2d	3b	4a	5c	6d	7b	8a
9d	10b	11d	12d	13a	14d	15a	16b
17c	18a	19a	20d	21a	22d	23c	24d
25d	26d	27a	28c	29c	30a		

NATIONAL AND INTERNATIONAL ORGANISATIONS

1c	2d	3a	4b	5c	6b	7a	8d
9c	10a	11b	12c	13d	14a	15b	16d
17a	18d	19c	20b	21d	22a	23c	24d
25b	26d	27a	28c	29d	30b		

ECONOMY AND BUSINESS

1c	2d	3a	4a	5b	6b	7d	8b
9c	10a	11c	12d	13a	14d	15d	16d
17a	18d	19a	20a	21c	22d	23c	24b
25d	26a	27a	28b	29c	30a		

RELIGIONS

1d	2c	3b	4c	5a	6c	7c	8d
9c	10a	11a	12b	13d	14b	15a	16b
17b	18a	19d	20c	21d	22c	23a	24c
25a	26b	27d	28d	29c	30a		

INDIAN HERITAGE AND CULTURE

1a	2d	3d	4c	5d	6c	7d	8b
9c	10b	11c	12a	13c	14d	15a	16d
17c	18c	19c	20d	21a	22c	23a	24d
25b	26a	27b	28b	29d	30b		

WORLD CULTURE

1d	2b	3b	4a	5d	6a	7b	8c
9d	10b	11c	12b	13b	14d	15c	16c
17a	18a	19c	20a	21c	22c	23d	24d
25c	26c	27d	28d	29c	30c		

INDIAN LITERATURE

1a	2c	3d	4c	5d	6d	7d	8d
9b	10c	11d	12a	13b	14c	15b	16c
17b	18a	19a	20c	21c	22d	23d	24a
25c	26a	27b	28a	29b	30a		

WORLD LITERATURE

1c	2b	3c	4a	5d	6b	7c	8b
9a	10c	11d	12b	13a	14c	15d	16a
17a	18c	19b	20c	21d	22b	23c	24a
25c	26a	27d	28d	29b	30b		

FAMOUS INDIANS

1b	2d	3d	4b	5d	6a	7a	8d
9b	10b	11d	12a	13a	14b	15d	16b
17c	18d	19a	20d	21c	22c	23b	24a
25d	26b	27c	28b	29b			

FAMOUS PEOPLE OF THE WORLD

1b	2c	3a	4a	5b	6d	7c	8a
9b	10c	11c	12b	13b	14a	15b	16c
17c	18a	19c	20c	21d	22c	23d	24a
25d	26b	27d	28b	29c	30b		

FIRST IN INDIA

1a	2a	3c	4b	5d	6b	7d	8a
9b	10d	11a	12b	13d	14c	15d	16b
17c	18b	19c	20c	21d	22d	23d	24b
25b	26b	27d	28a	29d	30b		

FIRST IN THE WORLD

1d	2b	3d	4a	5d	6b	7c	8a
9d	10c	11b	12c	13a	14c	15d	16b
17b	18c	19a	20d	21c	22a	23a	24b
25a	26c	27c	28b	29b	30d		

ENVIRONMENT

1d	2c	3b	4a	5b	6c	7c	8a
9b	10d	11a	12d	13b	14c	15c	16d
17b	18a	19c	20d	21a	22d	23c	24b
25d	26c	27d	28d	29b	30a		

INDIAN STATES

1a	2b	3d	4c	5a	6a	7c	8b
9c	10a	11b	12c	13a	14a	15b	16c
17d	18a	19b	20d	21d	22a	23b	24a
25d	26d	27b	28d	29b	30c		

NATIONS OF THE WORLD

1a	2c	3b	4c	5a	6c	7a	8a
9b	10c	11d	12c	13d	14a	15a	16a
17a	18d	19a	20d	21c	22b	23d	24b
25a	26a	27c	28d	29b	30a		

INDIAN SCIENCE

1d	2c	3a	4d	5b	6d	7b	8a
9d	10b	11b	12b	13d	14d	15b	16d
17c	18c	19c	20a	21a	22d	23c	24d
25c	26d	27c	28a	29d	30d		

PHYSICAL SCIENCES

1c	2c	3b	4d	5b	6a	7a	8d
9d	10c	11b	12b	13d	14d	15d	16c
17b	18b	19b	20a	21d	22c	23b	24a
25c	26c	27d	28a	29d	30a		

LIFE SCIENCES

1b	2d	3b	4c	5d	6d	7c	8c
9a	10d	11a	12b	13a	14c	15d	16a
17b	18c	19c	20a	21c	22a	23c	24a
25b	26a	27d	28a	29a	30a		

MEDICAL SCIENCES

1d	2c	3b	4d	5c	6d	7b	8b
9c	10a	11b	12d	13b	14a	15b	16a
17c	18d	19c	20d	21a	22b	23b	24a
25b	26a	27b	28d	29b	30c		

HEALTH AND NUTRITION

1d	2c	3c	4c	5c	6c	7b	8c
9a	10c	11a	12c	13b	14d	15d	16a
17c	18d	19b	20d	21b	22c	23a	24b
25a	26a	27d	28a	29b	30a		

TRANSPORT AND COMMUNICATION

1a	2b	3c	4c	5d	6d	7c	8c
9a	10c	11d	12a	13b	14a	15d	16c
17d	18c	19b	20d	21c	22a	23d	24d
25c	26c	27b	28d	29c	30d		

DISCOVERIES AND INVENTIONS

1d	2b	3d	4c	5d	6c	7d	8a
9d	10a	11c	12a	13a	14d	15d	16b
17d	18c	19c	20c	21d	22d	23a	24d
25a	26d	27c	28b	29b	30d		

ASTRONOMY AND UNIVERSE

1c	2a	3c	4c	5d	6b	7d	8a
9b	10c	11d	12c	13b	14d	15d	16a
17b	18d	19a	20d	21d	22b	23d	24b
25b	26d	27d	28b	29d	30c		

SPACE EXPLORATION

1a	2c	3d	4c	5a	6a	7b	8b
9a	10d	11c	12c	13a	14a	15b	16c
17d	18c	19a	20b	21d	22b	23a	24c
25c	26c	27b	28a	29c	30c		

NATIONAL AWARDS AND HONOURS

1a	2a	3d	4b	5b	6b	7c	8a
9d	10a	11a	12d	13a	14c	15a	16b
17c	18c	19d	20a	21c	22a	23b	24d
25a	26d	27d	28c	29a	30b		

INTERNATIONAL AWARDS AND HONOURS

1a	2b	3a	4c	5a	6b	7c	8d
9c	10c	11d	12d	13b	14d	15d	16b
17a	18c	19a	20c	21c	22a	23a	24a
25c	26d	27c	28c	29d	30a		

SPORTS IN INDIA

1d	2a	3d	4c	5c	6b	7d	8a
9b	10c	11b	12d	13a	14d	15a	16b
17b	18b	19a	20d	21d	22b	23c	24d
25b	26d	27d	28c	29c	30a		

WORLD OF SPORTS

1b	2c	3d	4b	5a	6b	7a	8a
9a	10b	11c	12b	13c	14c	15a	16c
17b	18b	19a	20d	21b	22c	23c	24a
25b	26d	27a	28c	29c	30d		

MISCELLANY

1a	2a	3c	4a	5d	6d	7b	8c
9c	10a	11b	12b	13a	14d	15a	16a
17c	18d	19d	20b	21b	22d	23c	24b
25a	26a	27d	28a	29b	30b		

Other titles by Bluejay

Distress to De-Stress: a practical guide to stress free living
Dr Sujatha Sharma, Dr Avdesh Sharma and Dr Ruchi Varma

Magic Mantras to a Pain-Free Back (with 60 b/w pictures)
Dr Yatish Agarwal and Dr A P Singh

Pursuit of Happiness: made easy
Rajendra Tandon

Mastering English from Day One
Kavita Kumar

Mahatma Gandhi: the Man and his Philisophy

Winning Personality: the magic key to success
F Oss

Brain Building for Achievement
Herbert N Casson

Cheiro's: language of the Hand

Indian Palmistry
J B Dale

How to Start a Business & Ignite your life:
A simple guide to combining business wisdom *with* passion
Ernesto Sirolli

Why You Can't Lose Weight:
A guide to solving your weight-loss puzzle
Dr Pamela Wartain Smith

Do This Get Rich!:
Twelve things you can do now to gain financial freedom
Jim Britt

Natural Birth Control: made simple
Barbara Kass-Annese

Manage your Manager: dos and don'ts @ work
Kriti